OUR RELIGIOUS TRADITIONS

BY

STERLING P. LAMPRECHT

HARVARD UNIVERSITY PRESS
CAMBRIDGE, MASSACHUSETTS
1950

LONDON : GEOFFREY CUMBERLEGE
OXFORD UNIVERSITY PRESS

To
E. T. L.

PREFACE

This book has as its purpose to promote understanding of the three great religious traditions of our western world — Judaism, Catholicism, and Protestantism.

Understanding will not mean that the respective contributions of the three traditions to the religious life of mankind will become any less distinctive than they now are. It is certainly not here regarded as preliminary to, or a means for, unity of organization among Jews, Catholics, and Protestants. Unity of organization may in fact be undesirable. Unity of organization would indeed be undesirable, if it were furthered by abandonment of, or even by lessened emphasis upon, the central ideas around which the religious traditions have developed.

Understanding will mean, however, that the respective contributions of the three traditions can be effectively maintained without clashes of animosity among the adherents and opponents of the traditions. Clashes do now often occur and are one cause which limits the leavening influence of religion in our contemporary society. Responsibility for these clashes rests about equally upon adherents and opponents of the traditions. The advocates often stress points which involve separation and antagonism; the opponents fasten their chief attention upon minor matters of particular difficulty. Both alike thus tend to overlook the distinctive ideas and the vital aspirations which, embedded in each of the traditions, could in more favorable circumstances animate men's consciences and prove fruitful in their actions. A juster evaluation of the central ideas of Judaism and Catholicism and Protestantism might liberate the idealism of these traditions for further profitable development and wider application than has ever yet been the case.

The author of this book can not trace the degree of indebtedness he has to many friends and teachers whose minds and lives have taught him much about religion. He can say quite sincerely that he owes much to students whose criticisms have made discussion of religion profitable to him. He wishes to thank the officers of the Ethical Culture Society in New York for an opportunity to present his interpretation of the religious traditions to stimulating audiences. He ventures to express his conviction that the three religious traditions, all of which go back for much of their inspiration to cultures of the eastern Mediterranean world, can be successfully appraised only in the light of that reasoned interpretation of human life which is the outstanding contribution of the Greek mind to western civilization.

S. P. L.

Amherst, Massachusetts
June 9, 1949

CONTENTS

I. INTRODUCTION 1

II. THE HERITAGE OF JUDAISM 8

III. THE GENIUS OF CATHOLICISM 30

IV. THE ADVENTURE OF PROTESTANTISM . . 57

V. CONCLUSION 77

OUR RELIGIOUS
TRADITIONS

I

INTRODUCTION

Ours is a historically minded age. Academic scholars and popular writers alike busy themselves with accounts and interpretations of the past. We have political histories, economic histories, literary histories, cultural histories, histories of morals, of religion, of education. Even the armed services in the last war attached professional historians to their staffs whose business it was to preserve records and to write narratives of the military activities. Great corporations employ historians to tell the story of their rise and development. Private foundations and government agencies establish repositories for documents, letters, journals, papers of many sorts, in order that future generations may have accurate information concerning our times. Of making many histories there is no end.

To be historically minded, if it be no guarantee, is at least one requisite condition of the gaining of wisdom. It is a mark of maturity in the individual, an index of sophistication in a society. For history has many uses. To survey the sweep of long periods in the rise and fall of empires, to compare different types of civilization, to accumulate curious details about men and institutions, to detect the irony, the pathos, the sublimity of the course of events — this is a perennial delight to the disciplined imagination. To discover the major forces which led up to any situation is to know the factors which will condition control of the situation. To determine causes is to enhance the possibility of producing desirable effects. To discern uniformities of sequence among events is — though here the speculative hazard is great — to establish laws of human development.

Another use of history, less often and less successfully pursued but quite fundamental to the enterprise of understanding, is to define the central meaning which is implicit in each of the great movements of human history. Plato long ago stated the nature of this kind of inquiry, though he put the point in language which is picturesquely poetical. Everything that occurs in space and time, he maintained, is but an instance of an idea. Each actual thing or event, however, may fail, indeed will almost certainly fail, to represent adequately the idea it instances. Ideas become muddied as they enter into the turmoil of the visible world. Events presuppose the ideas but always fall short of the full import of the ideas. Events, Plato ventured to say, participate in the ideas or imitate the ideas, even though they do not manifest all that the ideas ideally involve. Yet only by penetrating through the events to the ideas they partially express can we gain an understanding of the actual course of affairs.

The point Plato alluringly suggested can be stated in bald prose. The great movements of human history, the movements which endure through generations or centuries or sometimes even millenniums, have, in the very fact of their continuity through multiple changes, a central meaning or idea which is their essential nature. Countless illustrations can be given of this contention. One could seek to define the idea, for example, of the Holy Roman Empire: one could seek this even if he agreed with the late Lord Bryce that the Holy Roman Empire was neither holy nor Roman nor empire — indeed, Lord Bryce's judgment is preparatory to a just determination of what the Holy Roman Empire truly was. Or one could try to ascertain the idea of Americanism, not seeking to impose on the facts some personal preference as to what it ought to be, but finding in the facts what actually it has been; and success in that inquiry might then help to guide the formation of future policies. Or one could endeavor to determine the idea of the Republican Party or the Democratic Party, though the definitions, when justly formulated in the light of history, might not prove useful campaign material for those particular partisan organizations. John Henry Newman essayed to define the idea of a university; his conclusion may or may not have been sound, but the intent of his investigations remains a legitimate and requisite task if ever a university is to be understood. So a bank, a state, the British Empire, Jacksonian democracy, socialism, or any other historical movement can be interpreted as the visible expression of an idea which is its essential nature.

The most important of all the great historical movements in our western culture are the three institutionalized religious traditions, Judaism, Catholicism, and Protestantism. In them, much more than elsewhere, are apparent the aspirations for values which men have deemed of supreme worth. The pursuit of these values has never been serene and clear: it has been intertwined with, at times it has been overlaid by, a tangle of sordid lusts and blind impulses and base passions. But men have never lived by bread alone, even if bread be one of the inevitable objectives of their struggles. They have also lived in part by their visions of ideal perfection. And when they have so lived, loyalty to their visions has conditioned all their other activities: it has built an overarching framework within the structure of which their political and economic and military affairs have been contained. This idealistic factor in western culture has been, not simply another factor on a par with the various material factors, but, frequently if not always, a prior and controlling principle which has determined the fashion in which the other factors have found expression. Of men it has been said, By their fruits ye shall know them. Of societies it could with equal justice be said, By their religions ye shall judge them.

No other institutions of western culture have had so long a history. Judaism is three thousand years old; Catholicism is nearly two thousand; Protestantism, in some form or other, over four hundred. The ideas which these religions embody are more fundamental to western culture than any others. But these ideas are not necessarily identical with the professions which the adherents of the religions would be eager to assert. Great historical movements often come to mean something quite different from the purposes of their founders and from the faiths proclaimed at one time or another by their protagonists. Perhaps it will turn out that, in the case of these religions as elsewhere, men have builded better than they knew. Men's visions are often misty and obscure, and the meaning of their actions is not the same as their intent. Successive generations within one continuing tradition often have varied and sometimes have incompatible aspirations. Only an analysis of the actual historical course of the great religious movements can disclose what these movements really mean. Their histories have been extremely complex, but their intrinsic ideas are surprisingly simple. The intricacy of details in their long and checkered developments often obscure, even to historians who specialize in this field, the central and definitive ideas of the three religious movements.

The essential meaning of Judaism, for example, is historically expressed along with countless variations, countless deviations, countless betrayals, countless irrelevancies. Most students of Judaism have been engaged in narrating the story of these details; they have set themselves to a task that is proper and important. Yet their studies are but spadework for the subsequent evaluation of the meaning of Judaism as a historical movement through its three thousand years. Until the idea of Judaism is understood, the significance of the details can not be fully appreciated, nor can the essential be distinguished from the accidental. The same truth of course holds for Catholicism and Protestantism.

Culture, Matthew Arnold once wrote, is "a pursuit of our

total perfection by means of getting to know, on all the matters which most concern us, the best which has been thought and said in the world; and through this knowledge, turning a stream of fresh and free thought upon our stock notions and habits." This is a very particular sense of the word culture. Normally we include much more in speaking of the culture of any period or people: we mean all the characteristic ways by which men organize their living — their agricultural methods, their marriage customs and burial rites, their means of transportation, their habits of dress, their educational practices, their manners, their moral standards. But Arnold is more than justified in narrowing the meaning of the word to the specific sense he gives it. For a people's pursuit of their total perfection is what bestows, upon all their other cultural activities, much of the quality their living exhibits. Culture in Arnold's sense deeply affects all phases of culture in the broader sense. It points to the essential ideas which a society may be seeking to find means to carry out in actuality.

Further phrases in Arnold's definition are worthy of attention. Culture is not easily won. A man can not gain it by sitting down apart from others and spinning it out of his own resources through use of his own native powers. He who seeks to isolate himself from the social context of great historical movements succeeds only in impoverishing his living: that way lies barbarism, not culture. Men have often wished to cut loose from irksome restraints and outworn customs: they have at times profited, and will again often profit, by courageous independence of what they rightly call "the dead hand of the past." But in cutting loose from evil confinements of some particular oppressive situation, they need more than self-reliance. They need more than freedom from false notions and base routines. They need instruction. And there is no source of instruction more profitable than a broad and rich appropriation of "the best that has been thought and said in the world." Emancipation comes not by cutting oneself off from the past, but by increasing the range of one's social inheritance to include the best the past has to offer.

In other words, men gain culture by contact with the great traditions of their history. The term tradition, however, can not be safely used without comment upon its meaning. Too often it is used today as a term of reproach: the modern mind tends to confuse the traditional with the outworn. Actually, all men live under the influence of tradition: they speak and live as classicists or romanticists, as capitalists or socialists, as monarchists or democrats, as conservatives or liberals, as Christians or pagans, as Jews or Gentiles. There is no escape from tradition except to the vacuous mind. Emancipation from confining tradition is indeed something much to be desired; but such emancipation comes, not through escape from all tradition, but through wise choice of tradition and generous understanding of its proper rôle.

Acceptance of tradition as an indispensable means of spiritual nurture does not mean subservience to ideas already expressed or to practices already tried. He who basks in the warmth of an inherited or acquired tradition is merely and vainly sentimental, like the "unreconstructed" Southerner who vies with his pals in asserting an unswerving loyalty to a way of life that has perished. No man has properly appropriated a tradition until he can use it as a technique of criticism. He has not grasped its power until, through its instrumentality, he can, in Arnold's words, turn "a stream of fresh and free thought upon our stock notions and habits." No other resource has a power comparable to that of noble traditions. For traditions, at least great and living traditions, are, as has been said above, historical manifestations of ideas that transcend in meaning their inadequate expression in the past and the present. They are principles that have had partial realization but still require, for their fulfillment, that much more be yet brought to pass. They are directives, furnishing vital energies for all sorts of future creative achievements. Men have all senses animals have, and at least one other — the sense of continuity. They apprehend, in their more thoughtful moments, their indebtedness to a past and their responsibility to a future. John Erskine recently wrote that by tradition he means "nothing that cramps or confines, rather a continuity that ameliorates the loneliness of this world." This statement, charming and plaintive and poignant as it is, yet fails to do justice to the dynamic urge of tradition. Tradition provides a continuity which, in addition to ameliorating any possible loneliness, also enables us to utilize the best of our heritage for the enrichment of our future. Until the ideas which lie behind our greatest traditions are exhaustively expressed, tradition will remain the basic source of effective culture.

To use history to ascertain the central ideas of our long cultural history is, to employ a phrase of Fichte, the vocation of the scholar. Or, since the scholar has many other tasks also, it is one of his most important vocations. This vocation is exciting and should be profitable. On one of the stones at the entrance to the great Hall of Archives in Washington is chiseled the inscription: *What is past, is prologue.* Only if the scholar succeeds in laying bare the ideas intrinsic to the great historical movements of our culture can what is past be prolonged to moral enlightenment and progress.

II

THE HERITAGE OF JUDAISM

Judaism is by many centuries the most ancient of the three great religious traditions that have entered into and helped to form western culture. It has had a continuous history of more than three thousand years. Originally a cult of a few Semitic tribes, it became the official religion of a small nation; and upon the downfall of that nation's independent existence, it was carried with tender piety to other and distant lands. Today it is treasured by many millions of Jews and is practiced faithfully by many scores of congregations in Europe and America and even other continents. Persecution has but amalgamated its adherents into communities conscious of their common heritage. Once centered in the Temple at Jerusalem, it is now preserved in synagogues which spring up wherever any considerable number of Jews happen to live. Unlike the two great branches of Christianity, it has never been proclaimed with missionary zeal as a gospel for all mankind. It has been cultivated intensely among a chosen people rather than carried extensively to all peoples. It has none the less been a formative influence far beyond the limited numbers who loyally profess it. It provided Christianity with its Old Testament, its lofty ethical idealism, its theistic faith. It has always been a source of instruction to many who have crudely dared to despise it.

Throughout the vicissitudes of its long history, Judaism has exhibited a marked conformity to a persistent pattern of life. Most institutions which endure for even a few centuries change in character. Judaism, embodied in an institution so ancient that all others in western culture seem by contrast to be recent creations, has to an unusual degree circumvented the transforming hand of time. Ever since it spread from its homeland across the face of Europe, it has maintained, generation after generation, an amazing constancy of type. This constancy has been a logical consequence of the historical process through which Judaism originated.

There are in the Old Testament different accounts of the origin of Judaism. The most familiar of these is the one given in the opening chapter of the Book of Genesis. "In the beginning God created the heaven and the earth," established Adam and Eve in the Garden of Eden, and progressively disclosed to them and their descendants the laws by which he would govern mankind. This account became the accepted view of many Jews after about the eighth century B.C., and was taken over by Christians as their official belief. Its prevalence among both Jews and Christians is due in large part to the beauty of its poetic expression and to the historical chance that it forms the opening chapters of the Old Testament. But it is not the earliest account nor the one which gave to Judaism its distinguishing character. It was adopted by Jews from Babylonian sources long after Judaism had arisen and had been definitely molded by a quite different idea of the relation of man and God. It is a hymn, foreign in purport to the original basis of Judaism. It is a hymn in praise of the power and majesty of God. It has been more influential in determining the conception of Christianity than in fixing the fundamental ideas of Judaism.

A much earlier account of the origin of Judaism, and the one which is quite probably authentic, is hidden in a narrative in the Book of Exodus. According to this earlier account, Judaism began at Kadesh in the thirteenth century B.C. Kadesh is an oasis in the desert lands to the east of the Gulf of Suez. To Kadesh Moses had fled as a refugee from political terror in Egypt. There he had experienced a religious conversion, a conversion to the worship of a new god named Yahweh. From this god, he was convinced, he received guarantees of help: help both for himself personally and for the oppressed Jewish tribes he might through Yahweh's aid lead out from the bondage under which they were suffering in Egypt. In the fervid power of this conversion he returned to his people, became the leader under whom his people did actually escape from Egypt, and led his people back to Kadesh in order that they might, at the first known shrine of Yahweh, pledge their loyalty to their newly adopted god.

Quite probably the people whom Moses led to Kadesh were comparatively few in number: they were but a nucleus for the larger group who were eventually called "the twelve tribes of Israel" and came thus to constitute collectively what we think of as the Jewish people. There were many accessions of nomadic wanderers to the Jewish fold, as the Jews sojourned in the Arabian peninsula, infiltrated into Palestine, and gradually took over the country of Palestine as their homeland. But the story of the solemn agreement between Yahweh and Moses' little band became current among all the affiliated tribes and was regarded by all Jews as an important episode in their history. For practical purposes, then, it was Yahweh and the Jews who met at Kadesh and adopted one another.

Judaism thus had its origin in a covenant. The Jews chose Yahweh as their god, and Yahweh was believed to have chosen them as his people. Precisely what the covenant specified in the way of mutual obligations and advantages was differently stated at different times in the development of Judaism. These differences are important and will require consideration soon. The point of initial importance, however, is that, for the Jews, religion consisted in the fulfillment of an original covenant. No other religion rests upon a covenant as its basis. The gods of the Greeks conquered the world, ruled it, sometimes as buccaneer chieftains, sometimes as moral judges, but always as conquerors. The God of Christianity created the world, put man into the world, and assigned man his duties. Yahweh and the Jews deliberately chose one another and thus made covenant. Even when the Jews came later to incorporate the Babylonian story of creation into their cosmological speculations, they never allowed this story to alter their basic conception that their relations with Yahweh depended on a covenant freely made.

Now covenant entails obligation. It entails obligation of a far-reaching kind. It is more than a contract. Even a contract is a moral relationship, requiring that each party thereto fulfill the specific pledge made to the other. Contract, however, lapses when its terms have once been faithfully carried out. Covenant is a more lasting and an indefinitely expanding relationship. It is not so much a business contract as a friendship with all its possible and subtle ramifications of mutual involvedness. The fulfillment of one obligation or one series of obligations but binds the covenanting parties the more closely together, revealing the further interdependencies and personal privileges and duties of a sustaining and indissolvable tie. Covenant is for better or worse, for richer or poorer. It is not terminated even by death. Yahweh is portrayed as saying to Abraham, "I will establish my covenant between me and thee and thy seed after thee in their generations for an everlasting covenant." Covenant involves more than the persons present at the particular moment when it is first recognized. Its duration is as endless as time is continuous. It embraces successive generations in its bond, unless indeed there be an absolute break in time, so that no legacy is passed on, no results from the past ensue, no continuity of history can be discovered. It means the establishment of a community, a corporate entity, a society of the generations of men. Through it a people is brought together, not by accident, geographical or utilitarian, but by deliberate intent to carry out an ideal purpose and collectively to fulfill a program of expanding commitments.

It would be historically unreasonable to attribute to Moses, or to the Jews at Kadesh, any comprehension of the full moral implications of the covenant into which they chose to enter. That comprehension would come later, as bit by bit the course of events disclosed to sensitive minds the nature of their commitment. And in the prophets who successively proclaimed their messages to the Jews, such sensitive minds were fortunately to be found. These prophets were not, as Christians later supposed from their misreading of the Old Testament, men who foresaw the future. They were rather men who, with delicately attuned consciences, disclosed the ethical purport of a society founded in covenant. Dependence upon covenant led progressively to a belief that the moral factor will surely be the decisive factor in history. It fostered the conviction that, in the end and when all things have been considered, integrity of character is the most important force in the world, more important than the rise or fall of kingdoms, because it is indeed the reason why kingdoms rise and fall. Political policies, economic processes, social customs are all of them weighty considerations; but, back of these and fundamental to their respective rôles, is the moral purpose which demands of them that they be so molded as to conform to the implications of the basic covenant.

The history of Judaism can be viewed as a record of a growing awareness among the Jews of the moral consequences of the covenant upon which their social order was deemed to rest. Lapses from loyalty to the covenant were of course frequent: no society has ever lived up to the requirements of the highest moral sensitivities of its best leaders. But, time after time, the Jews' recognition of the covenant proved a decisive force in their development. In spite of the meandering course of social change, Judaism has preserved throughout its long history a faithful conformity to a controlling idea.

The idea of covenant was responsible for the gradual growth from monolatry to monotheism in the period between the twelfth and eighth centuries B.C. In the earlier part of this period, Yahweh was indeed the only god whom the Jews were entitled to worship, and the Jews were the only people to whom Yahweh was believed to have given his protection. But the supposition was common that there were other gods too, gods who were Yahweh's rivals and who legitimately received the worship of other peoples. Yahweh was purported to have delivered his people from the Egyptians. He would continue to grant his aid against their enemies. He would guarantee them much prosperity: flocks and herds and large families. He would lead them into a land flowing with milk and honey. And in return for these favors, he required from his people certain sacrifices of animals according to elaborately specified rituals, abstinence from some foods and preparation of other foods according to detailed prescriptions, strict observance of the rite of circumcision for all male children, and, in general, obedience to whatever was from time to time ostensibly his will. The dietary provisions and circumcision were not required because of hygienic or other utilitarian considerations: they were marks by means of which the extent of Yahweh's authority was closely defined and made known among men. As late as the time of David (about 1000 B.C.), the belief was still prevalent that Yahweh was but the particular god of a particular group of tribes. For when David was forced to flee from before the face of Saul, his complaint was primarily that he was being driven from Yahweh's domains into other territory where he would perforce have to serve strange gods. The well-known words of the First Commandment reflect this same monolatrous attitude. The injunction "Thou shalt have no other gods before me" did not question the existence of other gods for other peoples: it rather forbade the Jews to put their trust in other gods or to erect altars to other gods in Yahweh's shrines. Yahweh was "a jealous god," demanding the entire allegiance of his chosen people; but he was not the only god.

Then came the transformation of monolatry into genuine monotheism. This change was not the result of philosophical speculation. The Jews were not driven to monotheism, as some anthropologists have fancied, by brooding on the vastness of desert stretches; nor did they entertain any eighteenth-century-like conception of one embracing system of nature which would require one all-creative power. Monotheistic faith emerged among the Jews because of their moral experiences in facing the disasters which threatened them. Yahweh had to be conceived as powerful enough to ensure fulfillment of the covenant, powerful enough to protect his chosen people from dangers that lurked across the frontiers which separated the Jews from their neighbors. The prophetic utterances of Amos in the eighth century indicate the moral ground of Jewish monotheistic belief. Amos saw the wicked prosper. He saw that powerful men, both at home and abroad, were oppressing the poor, were stealing the little possessions of the humble, were enslaving the simple folk, and yet were thriving and waxing fat. He could not believe that the god of the covenant would tolerate the unpunished continuance of such evils. He therefore had to affirm that the power of Yahweh extended far beyond the boundaries of the Jewish nation. For Yahweh would surely fulfill his obligation under the covenant and would wreak his vengeance upon those who worked to set that covenant at nought. Consequently, Yahweh must exercise control over Tyre and Gaza, over Edom and Moab, over the farther stretches of heathen lands, and over the men who lived in distant places. He must indeed exceed other gods in power; or perhaps those other gods were nothing more than vain fancies of his deluded enemies.

Amos did not attempt any definition of the limits or the range of Yahweh's power. He was not philosophizing. But his intense moral earnestness had its philosophical implications. And these implications would become increasingly obvious as Jewish history brought the Jews into contact with more and more of the world about them. Not long after Amos other writers, partly in religious rhapsody and partly in cosmic poetry, would find it easy to affirm that Yahweh alone created the heaven and the earth, ordered the very stars in their courses, and enforced the provisions of his covenant upon all with whom the Jews had even distant relations. To the prophetic minds of the Jews, belief that the moral factor in history is the decisive factor entailed the consequent belief that God is sufficiently great to safeguard the working-out of all human destinies. The world must be such, and God must be such, as to guarantee that moral forces will finally prevail. Monotheism among the Jews thus ensued from faith that the covenant in which the religion of Yahweh originated was genuinely efficacious.

Another important development within Judaism likewise exhibits the determining influence of the idea of covenant. Judaism always centered in the conviction that the Jews were a chosen people. No event in history ever shook this faith. But events did alter radically the conception as to why or for what purpose they were chosen. The Jews had at first thought of themselves as chosen to receive privileges that were not granted to other nations. They had been delivered from the Egyptians. They expected to be granted protection against other enemies, victory in battle, and the spoils of conquest. In the words of an ancient Jewish writer, "Yahweh gave unto Israel all the land which he sware to give unto their fathers . . . There stood not a man of all their enemies before them; Yahweh delivered all their enemies into their hand." At the instigation of Joshua, Yahweh even held the sun still in the heavens, as one old legend puts the point, in order to give to the Jews sufficient time to finish the slaughter of the Amorites. As Yahweh was jealous of other gods and would not brook worship of his rivals, so he sought to exalt his chosen people at the expense of other peoples. The covenant entailed special favors on both sides.

The growth of monotheism made this partiality of God for the Jews a morally untenable position. The god of one tribe could indeed be partisan: the God of the whole world had to be just to all peoples. Yet this God of the whole world remained in special covenant relation to a chosen people. The covenant was a moral affair: it could not be directed to the plunder of many to enrich a few. If then the Jews are chosen, they must be chosen for a purpose that is ethically worthy. And just at this point the conscience of Judaism worked its way through to what is one of the most sublime principles in the Old Testament, indeed, in the religious literature of mankind. The idea of covenant between Yahweh and a specially chosen group had doubtless seemed to many Jews quite incompatible with attribution to Yahweh of equal concern in the fortunes of other nations. This idea, however, came eventually to be the very basis of the faith of Judaism in the world-wide range of Yahweh's moral purpose. God has chosen the Jews, to be sure; but he has chosen them to teach other nations, to serve in carrying knowledge of God to the ends of the earth, to witness through their very sufferings the justice and mercy of God. There thus emerged in the moral reflections of Judaism the principle of the Suffering Servant. An unknown prophet of about the sixth century (whose writings are incorporated in the last part of the Book of Isaiah) expressed this principle with moving eloquence.

Listen, O isles, unto me; and hearken, ye people, from far; the Lord hath called me from the womb; from the bowels of my mother hath he made mention of my name. And he hath made my mouth like a sharp sword; in the shadow of his hand hath he hid me, and made me a polished shaft; in his quiver hath he hid me;

and said unto me, Thou art my servant, O Israel, in whom I will be glorified.

These are not presumptuous words of a boastful individual: they are passionate utterances of a pious Jew who felt so keenly his involvement with his people that he naturally used the first person singular in speaking prophetically for them all and in their behalf.

The spirit of Yahweh is upon me; because the Lord hath anointed me to preach good tidings unto the meek; he hath sent me to bind up the brokenhearted, to proclaim liberty to the captives, and the opening of the prison to them that are bound.

And the glory of Yahweh shall be revealed, and all flesh shall see it together.

This great step toward a belief in human brotherhood was necessitated by the logic of the idea of covenant. Monotheism alone might well have lacked this particular prophetic note. Monotheism, of course, would require that God be conceived as just to every nation and to every man. But it would not by itself imply that any one group was called upon to accept any vicarious suffering for the rest of mankind. Had Judaism been weaned from the supposition of its origin in covenant, its monotheism might have been an abstract philosophical doctrine, and its moral teachings might have veered toward a *laissez-faire* equalitarianism. Only a monotheism which was erected upon the foundation of covenant could produce a faith in the deep moral concern of men everywhere in the destinies of all. Only such a monotheism could lead to a faith that all men, in addition to possessing equal rights under a common ruler, were bound together, through obligations of service, in pursuit of shared ends.

Throughout subsequent history, Judaism has continued to play the rôle of instructing the nations concerning the moral purport of human society. The Jews, in spite of many lapses into merely nationalistic or tribal exclusiveness, have over and over again fulfilled the mission assigned to them by the greatest of their prophets. It was from Judaism that the Christians learned the idea of atonement, the idea that only by freely and joyfully bearing the burden of others' sins can a person heal the ills of this sorry world. It was because they took over the idea of the Suffering Servant that Christians could view the life of Jesus, not as a local tragedy, but as the embodiment of a universally valid principle, the principle of the power of redeeming love to remedy the terrible consequences of human sin. Among modern philosophers it was the Jew Spinoza who most notably expressed in his *Ethics* the conviction that all men everywhere are involved in one common and integral structure of society. In its faithfulness to the idea of covenant, Judaism has contributed to the development of western culture many of its most profound moral insights.

Judaism has not been without its factional divisions. In the days of Roman conquest, for example, there were various parties within Judaism which represented quite different ways of thinking about the covenant and about the kind of life which the covenant made it incumbent upon Jews to live. These parties had rival conceptions of Judaism. The issues on which they took opposed sides were momentous. These issues were momentous, not only for the future of Judaism, but for the future of all those peoples of western culture to whom Judaism remained through many long centuries a powerful ferment of moral and religious ideas and standards. Consideration of some of these parties is important for an understanding of what Judaism historically means.

One such party was the Essenes. They were mystics who sought to withdraw from the evils of the world and to carry out in isolated communities what they deemed the will of God. Like other ascetic groups at other times and in other religious traditions, they maintained their ceremonial purity at the cost of entering significantly into the larger course of events about them. They flourished for a time in a quiet fashion. But they gradually disappeared from history. They would have made of Judaism so subjective and private a religion that the potent idea of covenant would have been seriously impaired.

Another party was the Zealots. They were desperate patriots who remembered the temporary independence which the Jewish people had won under the leadership of the Maccabees. They favored armed rebellion against Roman dominion, confident that God would fortify their arms in a contest with even the greatest military empire in the world. They would "force the hand of God," believing that, if they but relied on ancient promises of succor, God would intervene with miraculous power to wipe their enemies off the face of the earth. Sporadic attempts to carry out this program led to occasional rioting which was ruthlessly suppressed by the Roman soldiery. The Zealots supposed that the covenant would enable them to count on supernatural might to reinforce their natural weapons. They gave the covenant a magical instead of a moral interpretation. They proved to be entertaining a mistaken view of history.

A third party was the Sadducees. They were aristocrats who sought to preserve the priestly rule which had centered in the Temple at Jerusalem. They were strict nativists. They opposed all foreign influences in religion and in society, and sought to purge Judaism from the infiltration of Greek ideas. A few of their more radical number seem to have joined the Zealots in appeals to arms. But most of them looked to more exclusively religious means to accomplish their ends. They regarded the ill fortunes of the Jews as God's punishment for their sins. They believed that more loyal compliance with the requirements of the covenant (as expressed in the Old Testament Torah or Law) would bring about a restoration of the ancient priestly rule. They thought of the covenant as a definite contract of mutual support between God and the Jews, a contract which had been adequately defined in the past and needed only renewed observance to make it prevail. Theirs was a nostalgic faith in a priestly theocracy such as had really not existed in even that past which they dreamed about and plaintively idealized. They disappeared as a party within Judaism when the Temple was destroyed in the first century of the Christian era. History did not move in accord with their hopes.

The Pharisees were a party of more importance because the course of events happened to confirm their faith, or at least not to destroy it. Unlike Zealots and Sadducees, they had no specific political program. They looked forward, as all good Jews did, to eventual restoration of Jewish independence and prosperity. But their concern was not to push some particular program for that restoration, but to prepare themselves morally and religiously for participation in the restored Jewish nation whenever, in the due time of God, that restoration might come about. They were, as their name signifies, the pious. They believed that, whatever the fortunes of the Jewish people might be, the primary rôle of Judaism was to cultivate in its adherents the kind of character which the covenant made incumbent upon them. Participating in the world, buying and selling, marrying and giving in marriage, ruling and submitting to such rule as was imposed upon them, they yet sought to be not of the world worldly. They neither fled from the world nor conformed to it. They interpreted the covenant, not as involving any given fortune in the world, but as requiring of the faithful, no matter what fortune might come, a loyal fulfillment of God's will.

The picture of the Pharisees in the New Testament is a quite different and very hostile one. Jesus is portrayed as pouring his wrath upon the Pharisees, calling them whited sepulchres full of dead men's bones, hypocrites who "pay tithe of mint and anise and cummin, and have omitted the weightier matters of the law, judgment, mercy, and faith." His indictment is terrifically severe: it may well have been in large part just as regards those particular Pharisees with whom he came in contact. In estimating the fairness of the New Testament appraisal of the Pharisees as a whole, however, two considerations ought to be kept in mind. In the first place, the New Testament narratives in their present form come from a period many years later than the death of Jesus, at least one generation later or even (in the case of the Gospel according to St. Matthew, where the strongest denunciations of the Pharisees are to be found) two generations later. And at this later time the antagonism between the followers of Jesus and the great body of the Jews had become acute. The denunciations probably reflect much of the later antagonism rather than report faithfully Jesus' actual words.

In the second place, Jesus had much in common with the better professions of the Pharisees and shared the lofty ideal of their better representatives. Jesus was indeed not a Christian, but a Jew. He was a Jew who founded his faith on the Old Testament and sought to prepare his hearers and followers, as did the Pharisees, for a share in the Kingdom of God. He had no conception of founding a new religion, of breaking with historic Judaism; he borrowed his every teaching from the Old Testament, criticizing the less acceptable parts of the Old Testament by the insights of its better parts. His quarrel with the Pharisees had the bitterness of a family quarrel. It was directed not against the Pharisaic ideal, but against the woeful performance of some Pharisees who, just because their ideal was so high, deserved castigation for their lapses from that ideal. It would be fairer to take Jesus' teachings as carrying out the purposes of the Pharisaic movement, than to regard his denunciations as a final judgment upon that movement. Jesus had a most unerring conscience in his interpretation of the

significance of the covenant; he may well have excelled all the
Pharisees of his time in the sensitiveness of his moral discern-
ments. He also seems to have had far more imagination than
they had, in his attitude toward historic Judaism: he com-
pletely neglected, if he did not explicitly reject, all the ancient
emphases of Judaism upon sacrificial ceremonies, dietary rituals, and other such externals. He may well have been far in
advance of the Pharisaism of his time; but, if that be the case,
he was not so much a foe of its purpose as a guide who carried
through that purpose with a power that made the less penetrating Pharisees seem his opponents.

The ministry of Jesus, if it is portrayed historically and not
interpreted dogmatically in the light of later Christian developments, was a reform movement within Judaism. It sought to
bring to the Jews a realization of the highest moral requirements of a religion founded on covenant. It belongs with the
labors of Essenes and Zealots, of Sadducees and Pharisees, as
an effort to determine, in the troubled time of Roman occupa-
tion, what precisely the covenant ought to mean for the Jewish people in their relation to the world around them.

The future belonged to the Pharisees and to the followers of
Jesus. The other movements proved backwashes in the stream
of Jewish history. But the future belonged to these two groups
in quite different fashions. The followers of Jesus, some of
them quite reluctantly and all of them without prevision of the
amazing effects that would come from their efforts, came to
break with Judaism and found themselves engaged in spreading
a gospel which borrowed much from Judaism but stood on a
different basis and symbolized a wholly different idea. Pharisaism, on the other hand, preserved Judaism intact, in spite of
the misfortunes encountered. It became the agency by which
Judaism was transmitted and continued. It owed this momentous rôle to the circumstances in which the Diaspora
occurred.

Diaspora is the Greek word for scattering. It is used to denote that particular scattering of the Jews which occurred in the last centuries B.C. and the first century of the Christian era. Many Jews had been "carried into captivity," as the Old Testament account expresses it, with the fall of Jerusalem in the sixth century. Some of their descendants returned to their homeland two or three generations later, but more remained in Jewish colonies in the eastern river valleys. Then as successive misfortunes, military and political and economic, fell upon Jerusalem under Greek and Roman conquests, other bands of Jews migrated to the more populous cities of the Mediterranean world. In the first century after Christ the number and size of Jewish settlements made Jews important elements in the trading centers of Asia Minor, North Africa, Greece, and Rome itself.

Naturally these Jews carried their religion with them. And predominantly they were of the Pharisaic party. Zealots had revolted and perished, Essenes had retired to the desert and vanished, Sadducees had tied their fortunes to the Temple in Jerusalem and had no reason for survival after the destruction of that Temple in A.D. 70. Pharisees, however, were able to take their religious culture everywhere they went across the Roman Empire — their idea of the covenant, their moral standards, their sense of the ideal Jewish community which yet remained a bond among them as they scattered to north, west, and south. They had their sacred literature, and they could and did found synagogues in which to meet and to keep ever fresh the consciousness of their heritage of faith. This faith, in which they stood firmly with one another and in which they dutifully reared their children, proved a social cement which geographical distribution never weakened. The hostility of other peoples to them — for anti-Semitism is as old as Christianity and older — doubtless increased the feelings of kinship which Jew has had with Jew across the face of the Roman

Empire and the national states of modern times. But it did not produce these feelings. The feelings were rooted in the religion of covenant without which the Jews might well have been absorbed into the newly forming nations, as Romans were absorbed into the Latin countries of southwestern Europe, or as Saxons and Normans into the northern countries in more recent times. No other group in western culture has had the same cohesiveness, because no other group has had the same basis for its existence.

The triumph of Pharisaism within Judaism in the first century has had a decisive effect upon both Judaism and the whole of western culture. For it fixed the essential meaning of the covenant for the long course of the centuries from that time to our own day. Cut loose from what they have always continued to think of as their homeland, Jews have retained their ancestral faith and pieties as a finished form of religion. They have been devoted to its preservation, its transmission, its maintenance in what they have believed to be its pure form. The Diaspora ended the internal development of Judaism and sent it forth into the world as an established attitude toward life. Judaism is to its adherents a heritage to which they remain faithful with a loyalty which has preserved it through persecutions and other vicissitudes of history. Judaism is today close to what it was nearly two thousand years ago.

Now, in our own day, there is coming to pass a restoration of the Jews, or of some part of them, to their homeland. The Zionist movement of the last century is finding a kind of fulfillment in the establishment of the nation of Israel. That movement has had many and mixed motivations. But its strength has come, not so much from the basic faith of Jews in the moral significance of the covenant, as from the acute needs of modern Jews to escape dire persecutions and even threats of extermination. Agitation for the creation of the Israeli state has rather obscured than clarified the problem of Judaism.

Thousands of Jews have returned and thousands more may yet return to Palestine. But the millions of Jews who live today in Europe and America will probably mostly continue to live in the lands where their worldly interests lie. They are tied to western countries by language, by social habits, by commercial investments, by means of livelihood, by opportunities for education and development. The success of the Zionist movement may change the pattern of life for hundreds and thousands: it will leave things comparatively unchanged for millions.

Judaism today faces a crisis of stupendous nature. Judaism, it might fairly be said, faces a greater crisis than do the Jews. Jews, aside from those who join the Zionist movement, are often seeking to survive in the modern world as citizens who in their respective nations become akin to the non-Jewish citizens of these nations. But the amalgamation of Jews into the modern world, with no distinguishing cultural marks, would mean the end of Judaism and of that mission which it has ever been the historic destiny of Judaism to maintain. The problem of Jews in the twentieth century may be to discover what measure of justice they may win without racial discrimination. The problem of Judaism, however, is utterly different. It is rather to discover whether the heritage of the religion of covenant can be preserved with undiminished power in the midst of the accelerated changes that modern civilization has promoted and is still promoting. And this latter problem is one that concerns all peoples everywhere, Jew and Gentile alike, whether they be conscious of it or not.

And, strangely enough, one of the most ironic facts of religious history is that the constitution of Judaism is itself one of the chief difficulties in the way of a happy solution to the problem of Judaism. The very idea of an ideal community, a distinctive community with its separate practices, has so tied together the Jews of three thousand years of history that Jews today often confuse the moral realities of the covenant with ancient rituals and taboos which are utterly anachronistic in modern civilization. Jews have through the centuries been amazingly loyal to the covenant. They have often of course failed to see their ideals clearly or to fulfill duly the ideals they have seen. But in their deviations from the full meaning of the central idea of their faith, they have probably offended far less than the rank and file of the other religious traditions of our western culture. The trouble lies elsewhere than in the delinquencies of which Jews, like all men, are at all times prone to be guilty.

The trouble lies in close dependence upon what has been the source of Judaism's greatest worth to mankind. If the Diaspora so fixed the meaning of the idea of covenant as to make it an outstanding contribution to the ethical thinking and moral performance of western culture, it also fixed within Judaism for all subsequent generations many beliefs and practices which time might otherwise have disclosed and corrected. It carried the religion of covenant to many lands, but it also fostered the supposition that Judaism was already complete as it ventured abroad and away from the home of its birth. Hence the covenant was unfortunately regarded as dependent upon continuance of archaic elements associated with it in bygone days. Devotion to the heritage of the covenant has therefore been accompanied, for most Jews and at most times, with insistence on circumcision as a mark of holiness, with attention to dietary regulations as preliminary to sharing in the community of the faith, with celebration of feasts the origin of which has long since been forgotten and the observance of which is therefore a matter of mechanical punctiliousness instead of liberation of spirit. In Judaism the essential and the extraneous are more intimately and more tragically mixed than perhaps anywhere else in the confused maze of western culture.

One of the most significant facts about Judaism is that it (unlike Christianity, Mohammedanism, Mormonism, Buddhism) has never been a missionary religion. Universal in the import of its central idea, it has yet remained narrowly racial in its appeal. A good Jew would never urge others to become a Jew: rather he would earnestly warn a prospective convert of the many difficulties in his way. A confession of faith can not make a Gentile into a Jew. To be a Jew, one must live in the Jewish way — that is, one must sincerely accept all the archaic features as well as the central idea of Judaism. Even wholehearted proponents of Judaism have seemingly had a dim realization of the impasse their religion presents to men. For while rejoicing with pride in the contribution which Judaism has made to history, they have never had the ambition of making Judaism into a universal religion for the world. In this respect they are unique and in contrast to the zealous advocates of other faiths.

During the last century certain pious Jews have inaugurated reform movements to meet what has here been called the problem of Judaism. Orthodox Judaism still holds the allegiance of the great mass of Jews. But Reform Judaism and Conservative Judaism have sought to adjust the ancestral faith to the advances in knowledge which have come about in modern times. The latter group would preserve the great ideals and the significant cultural contributions of Judaism, treating the anachronistic curiosities of orthodox Judaism not as essential conditions for acceptance of the moral purport of the covenant, but as symbols of the historic continuity of the faith through the centuries. The former group, however, has made a more distinct break with the past, treating the orthodox rites as superstitions which they are themselves proud to have outgrown. The Emancipation, as Reform Jews name their movement, aimed to discard the untenable errors of primitive times and yet to preserve the permanently important features of the historic faith. But here as elsewhere in social life, the ruthless pulling up of weeds has disturbed the roots of those plants which were to be retained. A disruption of Judaism has recently been threatened which impairs that sense of mutual involvement of all Jews in one anothers' destinies which had sustained Judaism as a powerful force through earlier centuries. Reform may have been needed to attune Judaism to currents of modern life. But it has also purchased its gain at a price, the price of weakening sensitivity to the basic idea of covenant. Reform Judaism is more akin to a Protestant sect than to the historic faith out of which it has grown. It has reacted upon even orthodox Judaism as a dissolving influence. More and more in the western world, orthodox Jews themselves take their religious traditions lightly. Many of them turn to Judaism only on special occasions like weddings, funerals, and the Passover. Along with abandonment of ancient prohibitions against shaving or against a mixture of materials in one's clothing, along with sacrifice of the quietude of the Sabbath in order to keep business establishments open for competition with Gentiles on Saturday, along with failure outside of a few metropolitan centers to carry out the dietary provisions of the Torah — along with such religiously inconsequential changes, there has gone a loss of feeling for the ideal community of all Jews under the covenant.

The problem of Judaism has yet to be solved effectively. It has perhaps been solved here and there, for this particular Jew or that particular Jew. It has not been solved for the body of Jews; and it is only through the unity of the body of Jews that the problem can be so solved as to preserve for Judaism a maintenance of the mission it has for centuries carried on in the world. Unless that mission is fulfilled, the world will suffer an irreparable loss. At no period in the development of western culture have men more needed an effective demonstration of how life is qualified when it is lived in the light of a recognition of the way in which all men are bound by covenant in an embracing unity. Judaism for three thousand years has been working out the implications of its fundamental idea. In spite of the confusions which have attended its presentation of that idea, it has been a spiritual leaven wherever it has spread. Preservation of its heritage is a moral need of Jew and Gentile alike today.

III

THE GENIUS OF CATHOLICISM

"This is the Catholic faith: which except a man believe faithfully, he can not be saved." These unhesitating words occur, like a cry of triumph, near the close of the Athanasian creed, one of the great creeds of Christendom. They were proclaimed, near the end of the fourth century or early in the fifth, in the confident assurance that the confused struggles of the early Christians, struggles both against a hostile world and among themselves, were becoming ordered by the growing power and majesty of the Roman Catholic Church. They express forcefully, but not indeed without some equivocation, a character which historically Roman Catholicism has exhibited through all subsequent centuries and still exhibits in American life today.

The words sound harsh and arrogant to non-Catholic ears. They have at times been uttered harshly and arrogantly, and have been enforced with too uncompromising zeal. Wise and discerning Catholics would be the first to acknowledge that leaders of the Roman Catholic Church have not always uttered them appropriately and with sufficient understanding. The claim which the words set forth needs to be analyzed. For it may be taken to mean two things. And these two things, though associated throughout Catholic history, are quite distinguishable in idea. The claim needs to be rescued, both from the uncriticized enthusiasm of its too hasty protagonists, and also from the indignant vituperation of its too partisan foes. It combines, within the ancient phrasing of its simple formula, both a sound ideal and lofty purpose for the nurture of men, and also a plan of ecclesiastical control over men's thoughts and actions.

The Roman Catholic Church has the two adjectives, Roman and Catholic, in its official name. Their presence in the official name is due to preconceptions that do not greatly elucidate the fundamental character which the Church has actually had through history. The Church came to be called Roman, because it was the Bishop of Rome who gradually became chief among the bishops or Pope. It came to be called Catholic, because it claimed to be universal. In fact, however, it never has been universal. Christianity has never been the universal religion of mankind, and Catholicism is not now even the universal form of Christianity. The two words, Roman and Catholic, will therefore not be used in this discussion in the senses just mentioned. They will rather be used to designate fundamental characters which the Roman Catholic Church has when viewed in the light of its actual history. They will here be used to designate the two distinguishable ideas which it has sought, with varying degrees of success and failure, to bring together. Its Catholicism then is one thing and its Romanism quite another. Institutions often mean in their history, as was said above, things other than what they have officially been supposed to mean. The two words will thus acquire in this discussion meanings which the actual history of the Roman Catholic Church, when critically interpreted, seems to justify.

Catholicism, it should be clearly noted at the outset, is not identical with the religious position of the Roman Catholic Church. The many local groups of Christians became organized into a Catholic body during the early period of their history, that is, between the second and fifth centuries. But history seldom marches along one straight and direct path to a single goal. Even before the Catholicity of the Church was firmly established, another process had begun; and this process was even more conspicuously continued in the medieval and modern eras of the development of the Church. This other process, the Romanization of the Church, was different in aim and import from its Catholicity. The Church thus gradually became both Catholic and Roman, though its Romanism and its Catholicity, combined in one organization and alike manifest in that organization's policies, yet remain distinct principles.

The distinction between the Catholicity and the Romanism of the Roman Catholic Church can be justified by historical facts. One such fact is that there are in Christendom other Catholic churches than the Roman. There are the various branches of the Eastern or Orthodox Church. And in various Christian churches which are not uniformly Catholic, there are yet Catholic parties, such as the so-called High-churchmen within the Church of England and within the Episcopal Church in the United States. Catholicism is not even necessarily and intrinsically Christian: it might indeed appear in the historical development of other religious movements, if ever a kindred ideal were there clearly sought and expressed. Catholicity is a character which it is the purpose of this entire chapter to make clear. But a preliminary definition may here be given in general terms. Catholicity, then, is the character which any continuing organization might have if that organization sponsored and accomplished the formation of a great humane tradition which explicitly avoided the errors of opinion and morals into which men tend to wander, and which thus provided a breeding ground for the nurture of successive generations. A non-Christian religion could in this sense be Catholic, though it would be difficult to name one that has been such. Confucianism is perhaps the nearest non-Christian instance of Catholicity. Even a great institution of learning, not essentially religious in intent, could also in this same sense be Catholic, though it would probably be fitted to deal with only highly educated persons and would not serve as a guide to the great masses of mankind. Catholicity is, basically, a cultural enterprise: it provides a fund of wisdom, gleaned from generations of human experience, formed systematically into a pattern of ideas and feelings and practices, proffered to new generations as a corrective for their eccentricities and crudities. It is a technique for the transmission of what men have come to know about the necessary conditions for the achievement of human excellence.

Romanism is quite another matter. It is the character which a particular church acquired when it sought to succeed to the privileges of empire, to sway the minds of men by its imperial power, to use the instrumentalities of civil states for the ends of morality and religion. In the history of our western culture, Catholicism happens to be bound up with Christianity, and Romanism has been superimposed upon Catholicism. When men view and study the Roman Catholic Church, they should exercise caution to note what in its intricate structure and processes comes from its character as Catholic, and what comes from its character as Roman. Among the Roman elements in its massive complexity are its papal organization, its College of Cardinals, its claim to temporal power, its definitions of infallibility, its pomp and panoply, its splendor of ceremonies. Indeed, its Roman elements are so conspicuous in recent centuries that its Catholicity is somewhat obscured. The nurturing value of its Catholicity has been confused in practice with the coercive restraints of its Romanism.

The Church of Rome remains, when all criticisms have been voiced of it, the great Catholic institution of our western culture. If it has confused Catholicity with other factors in its organization, it has at least kept the ideal of Catholicity alive. To it our entire civilization owes an immeasurable debt.

Our concern in this chapter, however, is with the Catholicism of the Roman Catholic Church. Not even of this one character can anything of a complete sketch be given. Four episodes will be reviewed in the order of their historical oc-

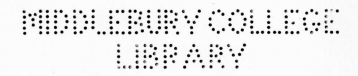

currence, in order to amplify and clarify the brief definition of Catholicism already given. These are all taken from the early centuries, when the Catholic nature of the Church was gradually emerging. Doubtless the selection of any four episodes out of many thousands is already an interpretation. But sheer chronicle is always an illusion. The barest or baldest statement of fact directs attention to one rather than another of the events which might be recorded. All history is interpretation and can not be other. One can not expect from a historian any method but the selection of such episodes as will make his interpretation clear.

The first episode to be discussed here is a change which occurred in the Christian way of life between the end of the first century and the third century. It was a change from primitive freedom to authoritative form. The early Christians were diverse in background and in faith. Some had been Jews; others knew little or nothing of Judaism. Some followed St. Paul in emphasis upon the indwelling Spirit; others relied upon the words of the historical Jesus or the moral part of the Old Testament law. Some looked for a speedy end of this world and recklessly made no provision for future needs; others provided shrewdly for the needs of more permanent and stable communities. Diverse moral practices frequently appeared. Prophets arose who regarded their "speaking with tongues," or inchoate babblings, as the voice of angels or of the Holy Spirit. Extremists claimed that they were possessed by the spirit of Christ and were therefore necessarily justified in all their acts. Ascetics advocated fasting and separation from the world as requisite to a Christian life, and endeavored to impose these practices upon other members of the Christian communities. Divergent beliefs and divergent ethical standards naturally marked a period when each body of Christians developed according to local preferences and had neither inclination nor opportunity to consult the customs and ideas of those in other

cities or provinces. The Christian world at the end of the first century was a loosely associated collection of persons who had perhaps a similar loyalty, but no integrated program of action and few common articles of faith.

As early as the middle of the first century, St. Paul faced the problem of establishing a seemly order in the various churches he had visited. He endeavored to introduce regulation into Christian living. But his technique for such regulation was not an easy one to apply in practice. It was an appeal to the spirit of Christ. And that appeal was not productive of the order he sought. For, as abundant experience soon showed, many sorts of inspiration could all claim to be in accord with that proffered sanction. St. Paul's principle was the inner witness of the spirit of Christ in a man's inner life; and, as such, it was too subjective. Some more precise definition of Christian standards, some more visible and objective measure, was requisite, if the more sober Christians were to succeed in establishing norms of faith and conformity of moral practice.

In ensuing generations several devices were formulated in turn, as successive leaders sought desperately for some means of promoting a more uniform and consistent Christian way of life. Some of these leaders, in order to make explicit what the spirit of Christ genuinely is, came to appeal to the words of the historical Jesus. And then, because various oral traditions were extant concerning these words, written records were prepared and circulated. But the written records were not themselves sufficiently definite. Different records were compiled in different places, under different oral traditions, and at different times. In the absence of anything like our printing, these records exhibited diversity of textual readings. Therefore the numerous records had to be examined, and the authentic and reliable ones had to be distinguished from the unacceptable and spurious ones.

Thus there emerged gradually a recognized body of allegedly authoritative writings which eventually became accepted as the canon of the New Testament. But even this canon proved insufficient to settle disputes. For the identical text could be and was easily interpreted in quite contradictory fashions by different readers. Just what would it mean in practice to obey such maxims as "Take no thought for the morrow" or "Blessed are the meek"? Written texts can never be final in authority when those who read them are not strictly of one mind.

A further appeal had therefore to be made beyond the text of the canon to some designated and responsible reader whose understanding might then be official. Naturally the reader thus selected was the bishop. Most Christian communities had a bishop. The bishop had only advisory capacity originally, as one of the oldest and most experienced men whose advice could be sought. But time vested him with increasing power. Early in the second century, St. Ignatius of Antioch went so far as to assert that no proper Christian could fail to honor the bishop. And to honor the bishop was, in practice, to submit obediently to the bishop. The bishop thus became in most Christian communities a living and decisive force for settlement of disputes within any single church.

Even that appeal, however, could not unify the Christian world and produce uniformity of faith and practice. For one bishop might well seem heretical or morally lax or unsound to another bishop. And, as a matter of historical fact, disagreements between or among bishops soon came to disturb the peace of Christendom. The next logical step in the quest for order was to refer all disputes to councils of bishops. Such councils could speak with finality. Thus it came to be generally recognized that full and entire authority rested in ecumenical councils, that is, in councils of all the bishops of the entire Christian world.

The development of episcopal authority and ecumenical

councils was not as linear and as direct as the simplified account just given might indicate. Protests against secularizing the Church were voiced loudly. Revolts broke out in behalf of primitive freedom. Individuals and small groups turned back to the witness of the Spirit within them. Dissatisfied bodies of Christians here and there seceded from episcopal control and interrupted the trend toward unity and conformity. But the trend was dominant and the issue was clear. By the end of the fourth century a Catholic structure was firmly built upon the foundations of primitive Christianity. Catholicism had come into being.

Catholicism had come into being in just the sense in which the word Catholic was defined at the outset of this chapter. Catholicism had come into being in so far as there was established a normative standard to correct the eccentricities of errant individuals and to moderate the fantasies of wayward groups. Its import was becoming obvious. It involved the conviction that men need more than enthusiasm and moral earnestness, that they need also regulation by a control they can not themselves spontaneously effect, that they become safely spiritual and truly redeemed only by entering into corporate relationship with a funded wisdom accumulated in the experience of the saints throughout the generations. If primitive Christianity furnished the enthusiasm and vitality of faith and morality, Catholicism provided the form which molded these materials into a wholesome and acceptable product.

But Romanizing was beginning too. Synchronously with the definition of norms went the growth of political control by appointed officials. The contention was that there had to be particular men to call ecumenical councils into session, to preside over the councils, to enforce the decisions of the councils. And the enforcement of decisions followed along the lines chosen by the men who chanced to be in power. Catholicism may have been, indeed was, the aim of the development; but Romanism was the method of implementation of this aim. Rome was of course the ancient capital of the Empire, and the Church at Rome was the largest and wealthiest of the Christian churches by the end of the second century. Church authorities at Rome felt a natural concern for the other Christian communities and assumed, and won, a burden of responsibility for the welfare of the Christian cause through the whole Mediterranean world. Particularly in the third, fourth, and fifth centuries, as political and military power passed into the hands of barbarian forces, the Bishop of Rome came more and more to be looked on as the last representative of the imperial glory and inherited some of the waning imperial prestige. Not until Innocent I in the early fifth century did any Pope clearly enunciate the position that nothing could be done in East or West, in doctrine or in discipline, without the approval of Rome. But earlier bishops of Rome, even Clement I before the end of the first century, had implicitly anticipated Innocent's more bold and open proclamation of sovereign control.

The second episode to be here discussed is one which went on simultaneously with the first and was constantly interinvolved with the first in its occurrence. It is the process of the progressive formation of certain articles of Christian belief into the precise language of the creeds. The story of this episode is too long to give entire; but certain typical phases of the story may be singled out for illustrative purposes. The creeds stabilized and organized Christian belief, as the rise of ecumenical councils stabilized and organized a broad uniformity of Christian polity and practice.

From the early days of Christianity, from as early as the time of St. Paul, there were two quite different types of attitude among Christians toward the person of Jesus Christ. Some Christians regarded his as a man chosen of God to be the herald of a new religious regime, a teacher of outstanding merit, the greatest of the prophets. Others believed him to be a divine being, incarnate in human form during the earthly career of the historical Jesus, but preëxistent before his incarnation and restored to glorified status after his resurrection.

Both attitudes had their respective appeals. The former attitude presented a peculiarly moral appeal; for if Jesus Christ were man, his virtues, the beauty of his life, his achievement of a perfect character were a challenge to others who then too, though themselves but human, might likewise exhibit the same moral excellence. The latter attitude had a specifically religious appeal; for if Jesus Christ were god, his exalted status elicited worship and made him a source of more than human power for the redemption of mankind from misery and sin.

These two attitudes were often so expressed as to permit their advocates to live in unison with one another. But when they came to be maintained in extreme form, they were opposed to one another in hostile fashion. The former attitude lent itself to use by groups who are known as Judaizers. The Judaizers were those members of the early Christian communities who stood closest to the Judaism out of which the Christian movement had at first arisen. They wished to retain all the tenets of Judaism, such as the dietary provisions of the Old Testament law, the requirement of circumcision as a precondition of entrance for all males into the Christian brotherhood, the centrality of Jerusalem in religious life, the Jewish festivals. They were Jews with an added faith in Jesus as the latest and greatest of Jewish prophets. They often remained within the narrowly racial conception of religion and opposed foreign influences. They viewed the elevation of Jesus to divine status, particularly the assertions of his equality with God, as objectionable notions that had arisen under Greek influence, hence as blasphemous perversions of the traditions of their own ancient religious faith. To treat Jesus as a divine being was already, to their way of thinking, to have betrayed the purity of a tried and tested monotheism, to have conceived of a noble

Jewish leader in terms akin to those used by the Greeks for their gods, and hence to have abandoned religious sanity for fantastic foreign enthusiasms.

The latter attitude, which cherished faith in Jesus as divine, could not tolerate this parochial Judaistic position. It held that the Judaizers were too much bound to the past and had no share in the glorious future anticipated for Christianity. Christianity was, in their minds, not another cult within Judaism. It was not tied to one people, to one race, to one city, to one set of ancient customs. Indeed, Christianity had arisen, they claimed, as emancipation from all the particularisms and inadequacies of Judaism. Had not the Jews rejected Jesus Christ? And could they then expect to force their errors upon the new gospel of the risen and glorified Christ? Extremists on this side of the controversy went so far as to repudiate Judaism as a vicious distortion of truth and as deserving of entire repudiation. Among these extremists was Marcion, a presbyter of the Christian church at Rome in the second century; his eloquence won many converts. Other extremists were tied up with a widespread development of Greek thought which is known as Gnosticism. Marcionites and Christian Gnostics differed in many ways; but they agreed in making Jesus Christ so entirely divine as thereby to deny his humanity altogether. Christ for them was a purely spiritual being, with no element of materiality in his composition. Christ, they professed, was never truly man. Christ had only appeared as a man, in order to be visible and clearly revealed to mortal eyes. His seeming humanity was but appearance, not reality. Christ was never born, he never suffered, he never died — for, indeed, birth, suffering, and death could not happen to a god. Christ was not simply genuinely divine: he was entirely and only divine.

The Judaizers on the one hand and the Marcionites and Gnostics on the other hand caused much factionalism within the Christian communities, many bitter controversies, distraction from peaceful coöperation, struggle of party against party for office and for control of churches. The very order for the sake of which the Church had become Catholic was being jeopardized. Those who sympathized with the catholicizing of the Christian churches could hardly allow the theological issues to remain a constant source of animosity and confusion. Some regulation of belief was essential to unity of polity and moderation in practice. The Catholic Church was not prepared to formulate any complete summary of faith, any official synopsis of Catholic theology. But it could at least draw up a brief pledge, to be required of all who wished to enter into Christian fellowship. This pledge or confession of faith became a norm of faith or creed. The earliest form of this creed is known as the Old Roman Symbol: it was drawn up at Rome to stem the Marcionite movement, and so expressly denied the tenets of the Marcionites. In a slightly enlarged form it later became the Apostles' Creed which has remained through many centuries one of the basic professions of Christian principles. It explicitly asserts that Jesus Christ, though the son of God, was "born of the Virgin Mary, suffered under Pontius Pilate, was crucified, dead, and buried." It was not a compendium of Christian belief: indeed, Christian belief was still too varied on many points to permit compact summary. It was a polemic against extremists, particularly against the extremists of the locality where it was first formulated, that is, against Marcionites. It solved no theoretical difficulties; it explained no philosophical foundations of the faith. It did something more timely. It quite directly repudiated the errors of those enthusiasts who rejected the humanity of Jesus Christ. It sought to expel these enthusiasts from the brotherhood of the Catholic Church.

Similar and longer creeds were drawn up in succeeding centuries, notably the Nicene Creed and the Athanasian Creed.

These creeds, like the Old Roman Symbol and the Apostles' Creed, were formulated under pressure of events. Never perhaps, until the Council of Trent in post-Reformation days, did a council of bishops meet to consider the possibility of a complete and systematic statement of what the Christian faith is. Normally Christian leaders were too preoccupied with immediate issues to sit down meditatively and to draw up dispassionately the well-rounded outline of a comprehensive set of Christian beliefs. They were often thinkers, sometimes thinkers of ability. But they were busy with the manifold problems of defending the Church against a none too friendly imperial world and of ending bitter antagonisms within the Church. They were not theological theorists: they were driven in their reflections by urgent practical needs. If the statements of the Apostles' Creed drove the Judaistic and Gnostic extremists out of the Church, the words and phrases of the Creed also presented new theoretical problems to coming generations. The solution of old problems, in religious as always in political and economic and other human affairs, determined the conditions under which new problems would arise. If Jesus Christ was truly the son of God and truly human, how indeed was he related to "God the Father, creator of Heaven and earth"? How also was the person of Christ, with his dual nature of divinity and humanity, to be understood? Men arise in every generation who feel bound to seek to make clear and intelligible the faith which is within them. And these souls, honest in their speculations but preferring some lucid formula to the complex of moral and religious aspirations of the vast number of Christian adherents, tend normally to drift into views which would offend some other section of the Church and so to give rise to fresh controversies. If the leaders of the early Catholic Church had no leisure for disinterested philosophizing, they at least made it their business to keep watch over the welter of conflicting ideas which were being forcefully pressed upon the

Church, to seek some means of reconciling the contending parties, or, if that failed, to find some means of silencing the more clamorous of these parties. If authority could not convince all parties of the truth about God and Christ, it could at any rate keep the peace. It could do even more than this: it could point out the errors to be rejected and guide Christians toward some moderate type of belief which would appear to be a workable compromise.

Thus, in the two centuries which followed the formulation of the Apostles' Creed, new heresies arose and new creeds denied them. Adoptianists, as they were called, presented the theory that Jesus Christ was at first a purely human being and was then adopted by God for special purposes and deified at the end of his earthly career. Sabellius and his followers, the Sabellians, invented the theory that God the Father and God the Son and God the Spirit were three temporally successive rôles played by one and the same deity: that God as creator was the Father, that God as revealed in Christ was the Son, that God as a saving presence in men's lives was the Spirit. Adoptianists veered toward the condemned error of the Judaizers; Sabellians, toward the fancies of the Gnostics. Arius sought a mediating position: he acknowledged that Christ was a preëxistent supernatural being, but demoted him to a status inferior to that of God. This mediating position, however, satisfied neither those who were inspired by the beauty of Jesus' humanity nor those who gloried in the majesty of his divinity; it met the fate of repelling both the major schools of thought, and Arius became the most accursed heretic in Christian annals.

These events, complex in their occurrence, have yet a simple moral. The faith once for all delivered to the saints could not be summed up in any speculative formula. The leaders of the Church found that they had to work out its unification, not by a positive assertion of the truth, but by a negative rejection

of errors. And just this is what took place. The creeds may
sound like positive assertions to those who read them out of
historical context. The Nicene Creed, probably the work of
the second ecumenical council of Constantinople in 381, states
that Christ is "God of God . . . very God of very God . . .
of one substance with the Father," and also that he "was made
man, and was crucified also for us under Pontius Pilate . . .
suffered, and was buried." And the Athanasian Creed, the
product of some undetermined council of perhaps the next
generation, summons Christians to "believe and confess that
our Lord Jesus Christ, the Son of God, is God and Man . . .
perfect God and perfect Man." But there is, in these and other
approved phrases of the creeds, no theoretical solution of the
controversies which were troubling the Church. Rather, there
is emphatic denial that the Adoptianists were right and that
Sabellius and Arius were right. There is stern warning that
Christians could not go in any of the directions in which these
heresies were moving. There is explicit summons to hold to
established positions in spite of the difficulties of making one
consistent theory which would embrace the beliefs of the
Church in synoptic fashion. There is insistent claim that the
faith of the Church, if it transcend the powers of human reason to analyze, is yet a body of truth which the Church must
preserve in its totality and all Christians must accept with
humility.

Historians of the Church were once prone to say that the
formulation of the creeds marked the victory of philosophy
over religion. Exactly the opposite is the case. The heretics
were the philosophical minds who tried in one way or another
to rationalize Christian beliefs and to make the beliefs lucid to
the human mind. They always gained lucidity, however — in
so far as they gained it at all — by pursuing some selected principle to a logical outcome, thus purchasing simplicity at the
price of neglect of other interests which were primary to other

Christians. The Church has never deliberately wished to be the enemy of philosophy. But in becoming Catholic the Church maintained that it possessed a body of religious truth which had authority antecedently to the emergence of philosophical speculation and had validity independently of the varying results of those speculations. When the Church triumphed over the heretics, religion won a victory over philosophy. Philosophy might come and philosophy might go, but religion remained permanently in possession of a body of beliefs which depended on no human defense for their right to command assent. As an ecumenical council had the function of enlightening the meandering enthusiasms and vacillating sensitivities of human impulses, so the creeds had the function of correcting the doctrinaire bias and speculative imaginations of human minds.

The nature of Catholicism is again apparent in the outcome of this second episode. Reason as much as emotion, intellect as much as will, thought as much as action, need a breeding ground for the fashioning of eccentric fantasies into sane and sound understandings. The creeds, from the point of view of Catholicism, furnish this breeding ground. To reject the creeds is then to spurn the wise consensus of generations and to substitute therefor the proud isolation of an untutored individual. To stand within the framework of the creeds is to align onself with a formative body of tested truth. To profess the creeds is neither on the one hand to scorn the honest intellectual efforts of any individual thinkers, nor on the other hand to boast of already having complete understanding of even those matters on which the creeds express certain convictions. To profess the creeds is rather to place oneself in a tradition which has seen and rejected errors and which so holds to many truths that it at least leads in the direction of comprehensive understanding. Certain churchmen, to be sure, may find in the creeds a release from intellectual effort: orthodoxy has always been to some men an excuse for mental lethargy. But such of course is the abuse, not the essence, of Catholicism. In purport Catholicism means emancipation from personal follies through a vision which no one mortal alone possesses in his unaided judgment.

A third episode in Christian history carried the development of Catholicism further. This episode was the effective suppression of a new heresy that arose as a consequence of some very trying events in the third century. The heresy was due to the high-minded idealism of noble minds but, unchecked, would have destroyed the Catholic mission of the Church.

In the years 250 and 251 the Roman Emperor Decius promulgated a law that all inhabitants of the Empire must worship the Emperor as a god. The purpose behind this law was to enforce loyalty to Rome. There was no intent to crush the many religions which flourished in the far-flung provinces over which the Empire held sway. Rome had ever had the wise and generous policy of permitting diverse religious faiths to practice their cults without hindrance. The new law meant to continue this generous policy: it simply added the requirement that, along with other gods, the Emperor too be worshipped. And on most religions of the time this legal requirement imposed no great religious difficulty; for one more god was not burdensome to religions that already recognized many gods. But to Christians the new law spelled irreconcilable antagonism between religious loyalty and civil obedience.

Persecution followed inevitably upon the enforcement of Decius' new law. Especially did persecution of Christians occur in and about the city of Carthage in North Africa. Some Christians obeyed the law, poured out libations to the Emperor, and saved their lives and their fortunes. Others fled to the mountains until the force of the persecution died out. And still others defied the law and met martyrdom.

Then, as always with Roman persecutions of religion, the

purpose of the law seemed to be gained and the persecution ceased. The martyrs were praised, and the refugees from Roman terror straggled back. But what was to be done with those Christians who had lapsed from grace? The "lapsed," as they were called who had yielded to Roman force, wished in many cases to return to the Christian fold. Should the lapsed be readmitted and considered Christians in good standing? Should they be permitted to enjoy the sacraments and other offices of the Church?

Two schools of thought disputed the point. A strict party under the leadership of Novatian argued that the lapsed could not be welcomed once more into the Church. The Church, they claimed, must not compromise with the world. The Church must be kept pure. The Church was the body of the redeemed and included no sinners. And what sin was more offensive than apostasy? The Church might increase in numbers and in worldly power by opening its doors indiscriminately to everyone who wished to enter. But it would thereby also lose its soul, betray its divine mission, and indeed cease to be the true Church of Christ.

On the other hand, there was a moderate party under the leadership of St. Cyprian; and when his party received the support of Cornelius, Bishop of Rome, it was bound to win the controversy. St. Cyprian maintained that Novatian and his followers held a false idea of the Church. The Church is not the body of the redeemed. It is not a body of men of any kind, however good these men may be. It is the Church of God. It is a divine institution which has the mission of bringing grace and truth and salvation to mankind. It should open its doors wide to all men, to sinners as well as to saints, to humble and powerful, to rich and poor, to young and old, to those who are steady and faithful, and also to those who are weak and erring. It should open its doors to all men, not promising all of them salvation, not excusing apostasy or other sins, but hoping that through its ministrations salvation may come to many, and trusting in its own intrinsic purity to redeem many a sinner.

In this controversy we may see one of the greatest crises in Christian history. Novatian's idea of the Church was akin to the belief of certain primitive Christians, and clearly it is implicit in the attitude of not a few Protestant groups in modern times. But it is not reconcilable with the Catholic idea of a Church which, because it is pure in and of itself, can bring salvation to erring and sinning men. St. Cyprian's idea of the Church was one of the greatest acts of statesmanship in the annals of mankind. Novatian had asked the impossible, namely, that men find their salvation first and then afterwards be admitted to the Church. Or, if this be overstatement, Novatian asked that a Christian be required to persevere without blemish and be denied any second chance to gain salvation. Novatian had a noble intent but understood little psychology. And his idea, however high-minded, was far less magnificent than the idea of St. Cyprian. Doubtless St. Cyprian's idea seemed to Novatian lax and sordid; but Novatian's idea seemed to St. Cyprian narrow and spiritually unimaginative. St. Cyprian's statesmanship was not just the worldly (or Roman) prudence which foresaw that the Church would dwindle into insignificance if it proved too strict. It was also and chiefly the moral (or Catholic) wisdom which understood the need of sinful men for a channel of grace. He had the idea that the Church was, in his own words, the ark of salvation. He demanded that the Church be conceived as an institution so full of divine grace that it may embrace all men, pure and impure, in its fold and remain itself unsullied. He thereby defined the idea of the Church which alone would make it genuinely Catholic. He clearly distinguished the Church from all other institutions. Other institutions are formed when men come together for certain purposes: they are therefore consequent to the men who assemble to create them. But in the Church, he believed, men have an institution which is real prior to and independently of association together, which bestows on them a grace they can not provide for themselves, which transforms many of them by a power that without it they could never possess.

St. Cyprian's genius brought to explicit statement the idea of Catholicity which was latent in the development of episcopal organization and in the formation of the creeds. He made the Church aware of the nature of its progressively emerging Catholicity. He made the Church self-consciously Catholic. His idea of the Church made it defensible to say, made it even requisite to proclaim, that only a person who has the Church for his Mother can have God for his Father. He gave the theoretical foundation for the growing practice of putting the Church, with its norms of faith and morals, prior in authority to the beliefs and customs of individual men and social groups. In and through him, Catholicism became an effective force in human affairs.

A fourth episode soon came to complete the process of establishing Catholicity in the Church. This episode, like the third, was connected with a persecution of the Church by the Roman state. In 303 the Empire was again concerned to promote political loyalty. Under Diocletian the law was once more enacted that inhabitants of the Empire must worship the Emperor. A similar course of events ensued: worldly compromises, flights to safety, martyrdoms. And when at last the fury of persecution wore off, the Christians again sought to renew their religious life. But this time a new problem presented itself. For among the lapsed were certain priests. Hence, the old issue was now joined over a new and more acute point than the readmission of the laity who had lapsed. Could lapsed priests be permitted once more to officiate at the sacraments? This question of reinvestiture of the clergy aroused bitter opposition between contending parties.

Again, as half a century before, there were both a strict party and a moderate party. The strict party was headed by Donatus, who maintained the position that only men of pure and unblemished character could validly administer the sacraments of the Church. The Church must at least keep its own clergy above criticism if it would preserve intact the efficacy of its holy offices. Though sinners might be admitted to receive the benefits of the Church's ministrations, surely sinners could not be entrusted to transmit these benefits. The lapsed priests, through the heinous sin of apostasy, had demonstrated their unworthiness to continue in their priesthood.

The moderate party saw quickly the menace of this contention of the strict party. The demand for pure priests was obviously noble in intent, but it was impracticable in fact. The character of priests could not well be established with any final assurance. Public sins like apostasy during a persecution could of course be detected. But a host of possible private and secret sins would defy determination by the most intruding body of censors. Purity of the priests was certainly to be vigorously maintained by every means in the power of the Church. But the validity of the Church's offices must be defended on some other basis. If that validity were allowed to depend on the character of the officiating priests, no Christian could ever be assured of salvation. Simple Christians might trust some beloved priest for years, only to discover in the end that this priest's character had some serious moral defect. Security for the sacraments had to be put above the contingencies of human affairs.

The moderate party was thus led quite naturally to a position as momentous as it was logical. Without any laxness of moral attitude, the moderate party asserted that the validity of the sacraments and other offices of the Church was in no way affected by the character of the priests who administered those sacraments and offices. The validity was a consequence of the purity of the Church itself. And the Church was pure because it was a divine establishment, not a human contrivance. The office of priest was pure, whatever might be true of the character of the priest who held that office. As Noah's ark took both clean and unclean animals into its shelter, so the Church embraces both pure and impure persons within its fold. But the ark was not contaminated by the presence of the unclean animals, and similarly the Church is not sullied by the presence of sinful members or even sinful officials. An institution which depended for its moral and religious character upon the virtues or vices of its constituent members, these moderates pointed out, would vary in worth from generation to generation, and in no instance would rise above the average of those members. But in that case the Church could not be conceived as Catholic. A Catholic church brings to men, to saints and sinners alike, a grace and a salvation that saints and sinners receive without merit on their own part and without contribution by them to its origin or status. The Church is thus conceived as unique among institutions because it and it alone is Catholic. Donatism, the heresy named for Donatus, was one of the most seductive of heresies because its motivation was lofty. But it was properly regarded as deadly to the spirit of Catholicism.

The four episodes of Christian history which have here been sketched do not give an entire review of the formation of the Catholic Church, much less an account of the still more complex character of the Roman Catholic Church. Other events of Christian history added other elements to the intricate pattern which the Church acquired in the course of the almost two thousand years of its development. But these four episodes do point to that essential character which constitutes the genius of Catholicism. Viewed externally and historically, a Church becomes Catholic when it manifests three marks: a set of dogmas to reject which is to imperil one's chances of salvation; a system of sacraments which are the normal channel of grace to mankind; and an authoritative hierarchy of officials to define the dogmas and to administer the sacraments. But beyond these marks of Catholicity lies the fundamental Catholic idea. This idea is that there is needed a training ground, secure from the contingencies of human fortunes, within which and within which alone men may overcome the crudities of their original nature and be transformed into spiritual persons.

A requisite first step toward the understanding of Catholicism is then the realization that an institution, and only an institution, is that which can be essentially and intrinsically Catholic. Individuals become Catholic through devout acceptance of the Church; societies become Catholic in so far as their life is organized under the guidance of the Church. Catholicism centers in the Church. It centers in the Church because it sponsors the faith that the Church, however manifested in this or that historical series of events, is supreme above historical accidents and vicissitudes. It makes the Church prior in moral efficacy to both individual men and organized groups of men, because it brings them a means of salvation which they can not achieve through their own natural powers. The Church is thus a channel of grace. Without it men are untutored animals whose impulses and faculties will lead them into error and sin. With it men may rise to a life that is more than an evolution out of the native proclivities of men.

The point of the preceding paragraph must not be overstated. Catholics should not deny, Roman Catholics indeed in their official utterances have never denied, that certain men may, here and there, now and then, by some miracle which unaccountably occurs, receive grace and win salvation apart from the instrumentality of the Church. But such events are occasional, exceptional, and beyond the power of human skill to provide or to predict. The great majority of mankind, according to the Catholic idea, find in the Church the only proclaimed and humanly known means of grace and salvation. To turn from the Church is then deliberately to estrange oneself from reliable prospects of salvation. To accept the Church and to abide in its ministering guidance is, while not to be assured of salvation, yet to participate in the one reliable, efficacious source of saving grace.

The Catholic tradition with its claim of the indispensable rôle of the Church in the redemption of men rests upon a solid basis in human experience. Not all human experience indeed will support it. Much human experience runs counter to it. Judaism, as was shown above, teaches that the human conscience is awakened and human nature is uplifted through deep-seated attachment of men in covenant relation to an integral group. Protestantism, as will be pointed out later, makes salvation an experience which may come to the individual in his solitary independence. Catholicism, if not as ancient as Judaism nor as congenial to modernity as Protestantism, has yet dominated the most outstanding institution of western culture. And this institution, the Church of Rome, has survived while other institutions have arisen and fallen. Macaulay, himself a vigorous hater of the Roman Catholic Church, paid tribute to its longevity when he wrote that it would probably be still surviving when "some traveller from New Zealand shall, in the midst of a vast solitude, take his stand on a broken arch of London Bridge to sketch the ruins of St. Paul's." And a disinterested critic may well conjecture that it is the Catholicism, not the Romanism, of the Roman Catholic Church which has made it endure and outlive all the other institutions of Europe. Catholicism has, in its offer of a source of grace that is supreme above the vicissitudes of human events, a psychologically potent appeal.

All of the great positive religions of the world, with possibly the exception of Confucianism, if that be classified as a religion, have been rooted in a profound distrust of the natural capacities of mankind. But of all religions it is Christianity which most deeply expressed this distrust; and of the diverse forms of

Christianity it is Catholicism which maintains this distrust most consistently and continually. The Catholic genius has much appeal for those who uncompromisingly insist upon man's natural helplessness to save himself by efforts he can himself initiate and carry through. One does not need a cure unless one is suffering from a malady. In the Catholic theory (as in some Protestant theories, too) men are originally corrupt in all phases of their nature: their reasons are liable to error, their impulses are erratic, their affections are worldly, their ambitions are directed toward transient and ephemeral ends of the political and economic scramble for power and gain. From their own resources, whether they stand separately and aloof, or pool their destinies in collective participation in joint undertakings, they can not rise above the limitations of their native defects. In their most sophisticated and civilized associations they yet but manifest the crudeness of their natural endowments. Only through submission to the Catholicism of the Church can they enter into the heritage of grace. The Catholic Church is thus the breeding ground of true beliefs, of noble desires, of fine sentiments. The Catholic Church, as many of its advocates maintained in ancient days and still maintain today, is requisite as the agency which takes the raw material of human nature and transforms it into the finished product of the redeemed man. The Catholic Church brings to mankind a gift without which he would continue to flounder through an endless series of personal and social disasters.

Yet, when thus expressed, the claim of Catholicism sounds harsh. It sounds harsh because it is uttered in the voice of Romanism. It needs to be interpreted more graciously in order that its full human import may be realized. It needs to be distinguished from the Roman accretions with which, in the most important of the Catholic institutions of our European-American culture, it has been historically associated. Catholicism means authority, and the Church of Rome has turned this authority into domination. Catholicism means the vitality of tradition, and the Church of Rome has turned tradition into resistance to change and experiment and adventure. We do not need to view man as corrupt in all phases of his nature in order to appreciate the value of a body of sound and moderate ideas, and of sound and wise practices. The doctrine of original sin is as rooted in pathological melancholia as the idea of romantic goodness is dependent upon careless superficiality. Yet when freed from the Romanistic setting by which it has been historically accompanied, the idea of Catholicism has a great human import which no individual man and no social group can safely ignore.

Catholicism is the enterprise of establishing in some effective fashion a synthetic tradition which will embody the wisdom of the ages and the balance of an integrated human experience. The Catholic ideal has a significance which runs beyond any institution which has as yet partially expressed its meaning and beyond any consensus of judgment as yet integrated. Fully to understand the genius of Catholicism is at once to wish to rescue it from the clutches of its historical affiliations. Catholicism, freed from Romanism, would mean that there is need among men for a reservoir of cultural-moral-religious influences which would be prior in time and prior in authority to the emergence of individual and social desires and ambitions. From the supply of influences which flowed from this reservoir, men would obtain discipline for their wild notions and guidance in their fevered undertakings. It would not, when so freed, mistake its wisdom for either total or final truth. It would not claim to have ready-made solutions of human problems; it would, however, claim to have a fund of tested ideas on which to draw in working out solutions. It would minister to men at all crucial moments of human life — at birth, at marriage, at times of disaster, in hours of loss and suffering, and at the ever recurring round of daily confusions and moral bewilderments. And in thus ministering, it would lift men out of the turmoil of passions which distort and retard morally effective living, and would bring men gradually, and sometimes successfully, into the transformed spiritual life. Men have always needed nurture, bodily, mental, moral; the relations of men in family and community and state have always needed reconstruction in the light of a higher ideal.

Historically, Catholicism is most conspicuously found in the Roman Catholic Church. This particular Church has happened to be, as the result of accidents of its formative years, the heir in western culture of the aspirations of the Hebrews, the philosophy of the Greeks, the jurisprudence of the Romans; it came later to absorb much that was fine in medieval times and the Renaissance. But to suppose that any one institution, even this great institution of the Church of Rome, is the only agency, or the indispensable agency, which can express the genius of Catholicism — to suppose that Catholicism depends on Romanism — is at once to be false to that genius. Catholicism will as surely have a future as it has had a past. Understanding of its history may be the occasion of furthering understanding of its genius; and understanding of its genius may be the occasion of furthering some creative embodiment even more fully expressive of that genius.

IV

THE ADVENTURE OF PROTESTANTISM

Protestantism is a movement, or a group of kindred and yet independent movements, which may fairly be regarded as the religious expression of the modern temper. It began — if one single outward event be chosen as the beginning of what had long been brewing in men's minds and emotions — with Luther's posting of his Ninety-five Theses on the door of the church in Wittenberg in 1517. Earlier attempts had been made to stem the control of Rome over all phases of western culture. Outwardly, however, these attempts had all failed. Montanus in the second century, Waldo in the twelfth, Wyclif in the fourteenth, Hus in the fifteenth, had raised the banner of resistance to Rome, and the Albigenses in southern France had held out for some two hundred years. But not before Luther had any opposition to Rome proved able to maintain public and official existence over wide areas and to grow in strength with the centuries.

Protestantism has never been coextensive with Christendom, as was Catholicism for more than a millennium. Yet it has been a great power in the world, a molding influence upon the manners and ideas of many million people. It never obtained any momentum in Italy or Spain or most of Ireland, and has had but precarious footholds in France and Belgium. But it swept powerfully through most of the other countries of western Europe and has given a characteristic tempo to their active and vigorous life. It has been the dominant religious force in the United States from the landing of the Pilgrims in 1620 down through our own day. Its outstanding position in America has resulted from several reasons. On the one hand, the immigrants who settled most of the Atlantic seaboard were from Protestant sections of Europe; and they and their descendants, under English leadership and as a result of English victories over France and Spain, became the controlling power in the subsequent expansion to the west. But also, and perhaps more significantly, the men who made America were far from the centers of European political and religious authorities, were fearful of those authorities, and sought their own autonomous institutions and forms in politics and religion alike. The modern temper and the American way of life were both favorable to Protestantism. They both were restive, experimental, distrustful of tradition, a bit scornful of old creeds and ancient customs, ready to work out new solutions to new problems, confident in their own abilities. In such a world Catholicism was often dismissed before its genius was understood, and Protestantism was bound to succeed even if it was not always wise.

What, we may well ask, is the essential nature of this Protestantism which disrupted Christendom, perhaps irretrievably, more than four hundred years ago? Protestantism has had no unity of creed, no uniformity of polity, no generally accepted form of worship. It has been an extremely divisive force. No Protestant sect has been long established without soon splitting into subdivisions which in turn have broken up into further separate and often warring factions. Efforts have often been made to amalgamate Protestant groups into some semblance of coöperation against a common foe such as the Roman Catholic Church; but the ties thus tenuously established have not stemmed the emergence of new sects nor overcome the separatist trends among the loosely affiliated groups. The conspicuous character of Protestantism through the centuries and in our own day has been, a cynical critic might ironically say, a lack of common character. Or, to put the point in more moderate language, the common element in the host of Protestant groups is an insistence upon the right to be different. Readers of the United States census reports can cite countless curious facts about the many Protestant sects, such, for example, as the existence of thirty-nine independent organizations of Baptists in just one county in Tennessee. Even where it may be true, as with these thirty-nine Baptist groups, that the common name indicates some common beliefs or some common practices, it is also true that the differences among the groups have been the things that have seemed important enough to determine their separation into distinct organizations.

This very divisiveness is indeed the key to a just interpretation of the nature of Protestantism. Protestants are people who find it requisite to protest. The word *protest* must be understood, however, in its full import: it has a popular meaning today of a rather negative nature and also a more important meaning of a genuinely positive nature. Both these meanings will throw light upon what historically and currently Protestantism has been and is.

To protest, we are quick to say today, is to make an objection. There is much historical warrant for interpreting Protestantism in the light of this preliminary sense of the word. All Protestants, or nearly all, protest against the authority and against many of the doctrines and practices of the Roman Catholic Church. Lutherans trace their origin to just such a protest. Other Protestant groups, in addition to opposing Rome, found it requisite to protest against one another. Calvinists protested against certain features of Lutheranism; English Presbyterians protested against the Church of England; Independents or Congregationalists protested against Presbyterianism; Methodists protested against lack of fervor in the other churches; Unitarians protested against the rigidity of doctrine in even the Congregational churches; Universalists protested against the belief of other Protestant churches in hell and the eternal torment of the damned; and so on endlessly.

The Roman Catholic Church, in marked contrast to Protestant separatism, has sought to emphasize the common loyalties of Catholics on many points of faith and discipline, and to minimize points of difference as occurring on minor matters within the unified whole. But Protestant churches have tended to overlook a large body of common faith and interest, and to capitalize some peculiar point of difference as crucial enough to justify their breaking away from their fellows.

To protest has, however, a further and more fundamental meaning, a meaning which, if not in colloquial usage today, was indeed the primary meaning of the word at the time when Protestantism was first coming into power in the world. To protest is, by derivation, to appear as witness in behalf of something. It is therefore to make strong affirmation. Shakespeare (who was less than a century later than Luther and contemporary with the formation of many Protestant groups) used the word repeatedly in this sense. He wrote, in *The Merchant of Venice*, "I have a wife, whom, I protest, I love"; and in *Much Ado about Nothing*, "Do me right, or I will protest your cowardice"; and in *Hamlet*, "Madame, how like you this play? The lady protests too much, methinks." There is in these and other such passages no notion of making an objection. To protest is here to proclaim, to assert firmly, to maintain a strong position in the face of the world. It may of course then lead on to the making of objections against those who deny or defy one's proclamation. But basically the verb *to protest* means to stand forth before men in sure and determined, even possibly in defiant, declaration of a personal commitment by which one is willing to live and for which one is willing to die.

Protestantism, then, is the outcome of a hazard of individual commitment. And this fact discloses why Catholic and Protestant are in natural antithesis to each other. A Catholic, on the one hand, is a man who regards religion as so important that he dare not trust his unguided opinion in matters which concern his salvation, but chooses rather to submit his opinion to the authority of a great and tested tradition. A Protestant, on the other hand, is a man who regards religion as so important that he dare not allow any one else to fashion his opinions for him, but insists upon the right to work out his own salvation for himself. When a Protestant seeks to make explicit the conviction by which he will abide, he naturally comes to protest against the unacceptable restraints of groups which would draw him servilely into conformity with them. He stands apart, sufficient and alone in his individual integrity, often perhaps mistaken and foolish, but always brave and self-reliant. He may not know, but he is willing and eager to venture. And from this individualism of the Protestant follows quite inevitably the divisive character of Protestantism. There are naturally as many types of Protestant as there are kinds of person who take a Protestant attitude. In the case of Catholicism it is the Church which is essentially and primarily Catholic, and the individual becomes Catholic through entrance into and incorporation with the Church. But in the case of Protestantism it is the individual who is essentially and primarily Protestant, and a church or sect or group happens to be Protestant only where kindred souls, particularly when living under the threat of coercion from other groups, manage to sink their differences in order to increase their strength or to enjoy some degree of fellowship.

Martin Luther announced the fundamental principle of Protestantism in *The Liberty of a Christian Man* (1520), one of the earliest and perhaps the finest of all the writings that came from his prolific pen. He wrote these splendid words: "The Christian man is the most free lord of all, and subject to none." Later, to be sure, Luther hedged a good deal. The Peasants' War in 1525 and the wild excesses of the Anabaptists at Münster in the early 1530's led Luther to make damaging compromises, to retract the clear profession he had at first made of the Protestant idea. Perhaps his retreat to less worthy positions, positions that may have seemed prudent at the moment but are as confused as ever any compromise has been, is not to be entirely set down to Luther's weakness and lack of spiritual insight. It may have been partly due to the weakness and lack of spiritual insight in a world where men are too often unready for the exercise of liberty. But however this may be, the first proclamation by Luther of the Protestant principle has about it that fine and clean quality of both intellectual and moral discernment which is the mark of the loftiest aspiration of a sensitive and brave mind.

We ought to note that it was the Christian man for whom Luther claimed freedom. But this localization of freedom within the Christian religion is but an evidence of Luther's natural preoccupation with the immediate situation about him. The truly great ideas, even when announced in the context of some ephemeral qualifications, can not be confined to particular cultures, particular groups, particular centuries. A more richly cultivated mind than that of the rebellious Augustinian monk would have seen at once that freedom is a human, not just a Christian, prerogative. Protestantism is historically a Christian movement, but it is intrinsically much more. What was said above about Catholicism can be here justly said also of Protestantism. Protestantism is only accidentally Christian, because Luther and other Protestant leaders after him were concerned with the immediate issues of Christendom about them and had no knowledge of or training in the broader phases of human civilization. But the basic principle of Protestantism could arise and flourish in other cultures, whenever men were willing to stand forth in their several personalities and to hazard, each in turn, his salvation on the wisdom of his own judgments.

The interrelations of Catholicism and Protestantism, both historical and philosophical, are numerous and complex. Most of them indeed can not even be mentioned in brief compass. But to mention some will serve to make the essence of the two religious attitudes more precise. Actually, both principles have profited from their joint presence in our western civilization.

On the one hand, Catholicism can always gain power from the need of coping with incipient or overt Protestant revolts. Before the time of Luther, the Church of Rome did meet successfully the challenge in such movements as the attack of St. Francis of Assisi on the worldliness of the Church or the claim of St. Theresa to direct mystic union with God. Instead of so opposing these movements as to drive their leaders into schism and to impair the unity of the Church, it absorbed them into the Catholic synthesis and thereby enriched the tradition it had to transmit. The rise of Lutheranism and Calvinism and other Protestant groups in the sixteenth century forced the Church of Rome to clean house, to institute reforms, to purge its portals of shameful abuses, to define its own position, and so to become more fully self-conscious of its own intrinsic genius. But from the time when Protestant groups remained outside the Catholic Church as independent and hostile forces, the Church of Rome hardened its attitude toward novelties and failed to incorporate fresh insights into its organized interpretation of the ideal possibilities of human life. It has not proved equal to the obligations of its Catholicity. It has too often been fearful of new ideas as disturbances of its current equilibrium; it has condemned new ideas because they were new and not because they were erroneous. It has preferred to stand pat on the *status quo* already achieved. It has regarded novelty as treason to its stability instead of using it as means to its continued growth. It could have been much wiser, if it had been less Roman and more genuinely Catholic. In religion, as in other phases of human culture, a definitive tradition requires a host of separate ideas and suggestions in order then to build them into a massive and integrated structure. The richer the materials proffered to it for its synthesis, the stronger might its traditions become and the wiser its gospel for mankind. Unless it becomes more imaginative in dealing with the daring ideas of Protestant individuals, Catholicism will become rigid and prone to immature self-satisfaction. It will then exhibit an unfortunately inadequate understanding of its own mission and be engulfed in the Romanism with which it is associated.

On the other hand, Protestantism has always owed much to its Catholic origin and background. Protestant leaders from Luther to our own day have taken over much of Catholic wisdom: they have kept more than they have rejected. They did not start anew; they were not as independent of history as they sometimes supposed. The smaller and exotic Protestant sects are doubtless more detached from the sustaining strength of a long Christian heritage; but just because of this fact, these sects pay the price of having quite limited appeals and rather bizarre characters. The larger and stronger and more discerning Protestant groups owe more to Catholicism. Even were their claim true that they were returning to the pre-Catholic days of early Christianity, they owe to the Catholic Church not simply the transmission to them of this early material but also the form in which this early material came to be cast. And the indebtedness of Protestantism to Catholicism is even more apparent when one considers the Protestant idea rather than its historical record. For individualism without instruction is always flippant and cheap. A person may, like a majestic elm, rise freely toward the sky; but as the elm would not rise at all unless its roots went deep into the soil beneath it, so the person would not achieve high thoughts or lofty moral aspiration unless his roots went deep into the history behind him. Profitable novelty comes not to the mind that starts with its bare native resources, its subjective biases, its limited experience. It comes at a price, the price, namely, of wholesome breeding, of pro-

longed training, of abundant learning through vicarious experience. A Protestant who has no sense of his religious legacy
from the past is like a prospector for gold who digs in his own
small dark cellar: his chances of striking a rich vein of gold
are negligible.

The point of the preceding paragraph raises the major problem which Protestantism has always had to face, still faces, and,
necessarily, will always face. This problem is the nature of
freedom. Freedom is indeed always freedom *from* something,
some tyranny, some outworn custom. But it is also and always
equally freedom *to* something, some coveted achievement,
some aspiration for a better life. Pure freedom, if one may indeed use such a phrase, is vacuousness. To be free of everything is to be nothing at all. True freedom is opportunity; and
opportunity is possession of the right to turn, always *from* the
ground on which one already stands, *to* some chosen spot in
some chosen direction and at some chosen distance. A Protestant, as has already been pointed out, is one who not merely
objects to some restraint but also makes some proclamation of
positive import. He freely chooses, instead of abjectly accept-
ing, the position he will assert. He must then somehow and by
some means give content to his freedom. Whence does he gain
this content? In what fashion will he draw up his protest in
the face of the world?

As yet, no historian has ever written the story of Protestantism as a succession of means which various men in turn have
used to give content to their cherished freedom. This story,
when it is written, will reveal the readiness of many men to
embark on bold adventure. For Protestantism is essentially an
adventure. It emerges only when a brave and reliant soul
hazards all he is and has, in order to protest his personal faith
before the world. It is not a body of distilled wisdom accumulated generation after generation and tested by a wide consensus of the experience of the faithful. Rather, it is a fresh

vision of a unique individual imperiously proclaiming his commitment and seeking justification, if indeed he ever find such, not in the procedures of the past, but in a new order which he hopes creatively to bring about. Not all experiments prove successful, not all adventures bring happiness, not all Protestant professions advance the interests of the Kingdom of Heaven. But just as experiments and adventures must be tried before their issue can be known, so Protestant professions must be dared, dared in thought and action, before their contribution to religious life can be measured. The nature of Protestantism is such that no blueprint of its development can be given in advance. Each Protestant commitment is a positive assertion of an end sought and a course of action embarked upon. Whence do Protestants gain the vision of their ends and the plan of their respective courses? By what devices do they give content to the freedom with which they act?

The answers to this question about the content of Protestant faith are too numerous to be here reviewed. And doubtless new answers will have to be given if, as is altogether likely, Protestantism continues to develop. But some account of the major answers which mark Protestant history from Luther's day to our own will clarify the description here made of the essence of the Protestant position.

One answer is that the Protestant gains the content of his faith from the promptings within him of the Spirit. Not, to be sure, from his own spirit or his own capacities. Many a Protestant feels that the Spirit of God enters into him, takes possession of him, motivates him, impels him. Luther believed just this, when he first broke with ecclesiastical authority and ventured to stand against the established conformities of his day. We are justified, Luther preached, by faith. And faith for Luther, as for St. Paul, was not belief: it was a dynamic propulsion which a man feels within him and may interpret as a power imparted to him by the divine Spirit. Only he who is possessed by this Spirit, Luther maintained, can be in the favor of God. Faith will surely lead to good works, can indeed lead to nothing other than good works; but the vital faith, not the ensuing good works, is what justifies a man in the eyes of God.

Luther's position was not without Christian precedent. It seemed to him more novel than it was, largely perhaps because it had not been asserted effectively for centuries. But it was closely akin to that reliance upon the Spirit which many a Christian had had in the earliest days of Christian history and which the growth of the Catholic Church had found too unreliable, too flamboyant, too erratic, to permit as a criterion of religious truth. Longer experience in dealing with those who claimed to be his followers convinced Luther himself that the appeal to the Spirit was not safe. The Anabaptists appealed to the Spirit and, because they believed the Spirit to be within them, defended many sorts of deplorable acts — sexual license, political rebellion, and even murder. There are more spirits, Luther came to conclude, than the Spirit of God. Some test is therefore requisite to determine the worth of these spirits. Luther then went on to appeal to other criteria than the Spirit: actually he made loyalty to the movement he headed the decisive test. And here the leadership of Luther deteriorated to a very mean and mundane level. The high-minded inspiration of his first years gave way to an astute political maneuvering of worldly forces.

The initial faith of Luther did not disappear from Protestant annals with Luther's turn to less subjective means of implementing his revolt against Rome. Others have made sincere and unqualified appeal to the Spirit. Of these others, the Society of Friends is perhaps the most admirable. From the time of George Fox in the early seventeenth century to our own day the Quakers have won the admiration of many observers who yet have not accepted their commitment. Some of their number, to be sure, have gone to extremes which have proved ridiculous. Fox himself made a major religious issue of his unwillingness to remove his hat in the presence of the King; one of his female followers aroused indecent excitement by insisting on removing all clothes and walking abroad naked; John Underhill of Massachusetts Bay Colony excused his frequent lapses into incontinency on the grounds that he had received free grace from the Spirit. But these and other bizarre episodes are trivial in comparison with the long record of fine personal character and unstinting social service which can be cited as the normal consequence of Quaker faith in the power of the Spirit. Quakers have quite logically refused to adopt a set creed which would sum up the orthodoxy of their position. Their commitment is that religious truth and moral sensitivity come to each man through the Spirit dwelling within him; and for the activation of that Spirit there is and can be no substitute. But, though officially creedless, the Quakers have in Robert Barclay a spokesman who in 1678 sympathetically formulated a statement that remains a norm to which the life of Quakers generally conforms.

The testimony of the Spirit is that alone by which the true knowledge of God hath been, is, and can be only revealed . . . These inward revelations, which we make absolutely necessary for the building up of true faith, neither do nor can ever contradict the outward testimony of the Scriptures, or right and sound reason. Yet from hence it will not follow that these divine revelations are to be subjected to the examination either of the outward testimony of the Scriptures, or of the natural reason of man as to a more noble or certain rule or touchstone: for this divine revelation and inward illumination is that which is evident and clear of itself.

The danger of this position is that it veers toward sheer and merely curious eccentricity. That the Quakers have not often been guilty of falling into this danger testifies to their high quality of mind. But in theory the appeal to the indwelling Spirit is not a principle of regulation of the religious and moral life: it is virtually denial of the need of regulation. It promises little for the future development of Protestantism, however much the Quakers may continue to exhibit serenity, integrity, and social idealism.

A second means which Protestants have utilized to give content to Christian freedom is the text of Scripture. Here is doubtless a recognition of one of the greatest sources of instruction for the whole course of western civilization. The Bible is The Book. Luther turned to the Bible and translated it into German, that he might use it to check the too rampant effects of appeal to the Spirit. Calvin, however, rather than Luther, is the leader through whose teaching the Bible became the ultimate source whence large numbers of Protestants gained material for their profession of faith. Through the work of John Knox and the Scotch Presbyterians and the English Presbyterians who were the greatest power in England in the 1640's, through the Pilgrims and the Puritans, this principle has become a widespread faith in American life. It is not wholly in contradiction to the claim of guidance by the Spirit. It may be, indeed it has often been, coupled with that other claim. Presbyterians have generally maintained the two ideas in close conjunction: they have professed that the source of their faith is the working of the Spirit upon their minds when they have been seriously seeking to understand the Bible. Why the Spirit should choose, as this point of view supposes, to limit its operations to occasions when men happen to be reading the Bible, is a matter which it would be difficult to explain theoretically. There are other great books, even if the Bible be uniquely great. But, none the less, that confinement of the activities of the Spirit to readers of the Bible has been widely asserted. It was definitively expressed in the Westminster Confession which was drawn up by English Presbyterians in 1643 and is still the official doctrine of the Presbyterian Church in the United States.

We may be moved and induced by the testimony of the Church to a high and reverend esteem of the Holy Scripture, and the heavenliness of the matter, the efficacy of the doctrine, the majesty of the style, the consent of all the parts, the scope of the whole, (which is to give all glory to God,) the full discovery it makes of the only way of man's salvation, the many other incomparable excellencies, and the entire perfection thereof, are arguments whereby it doth abundantly evidence itself to be the word of God; yet, notwithstanding, our full persuasion and assurance of the infallible truth, and divine authority thereof, is from the inward work of the Holy Spirit, bearing witness by and with the word in our hearts.

Nothing in the history of Protestantism has had more beneficial effects upon men and women than the loving regard in which the Bible has been held, the careful reading of large parts of the book, the memorization of many of its most beautiful passages. The poetry of the Psalms, the Beatitudes, the eloquence of Isaiah and other Hebrew prophecies, the portrayal of the character of Jesus, these and other parts of the Bible have been food and drink to Protestant minds and have given to Protestant worship and meditation a prime material of high spiritual nurture. Without the Bible Protestantism could hardly have survived, have leavened human lives richly, have kept to a wholesome course in spite of all sorts of inadequate theologies and barbaric notions, and have cultivated high integrity, noble devotion, and much sound morality.

But the greatest of books, like the greatest of blessings, can be abused. Elevation of the Bible into an inerrant authority on all matters has often made it an obstacle to religious advance. Appeal to the Bible as the ultimate guarantee of true faith, however pious in intent, has in practice amounted to obstinate insistence on the right to be historically illiterate. Instead of promoting wisdom, it has too often fostered a fanatical obscurantism. The "Bible Belt" in the United States has done more than impede the teaching of modern biology and an understanding of the place and scope of scientific inquiry. It has also cultivated religious bigotry and moral immaturity. Uncritical allegiance to the Bible has brought religion into disrepute as inimical to a sound scholarship. It has led men to wrest some phrases of Scripture from their context and to build up doctrines (such as original sin or a capricious deity who interferes miraculously with the natural sequence of cause and effect) which a better grasp of physics and psychology would render untenable. It has frequently gone hand in hand with reactionary notions which view human virtue in terms of merely negative abstention from alcoholic drink, card-playing, attendance at dances or theaters. This reactionary morality can hardly be blamed on the Bible; but there is significance in the fact that those who treat the Bible as an ultimate authority are also often capable of entertaining these absurd moral tenets. When one reviews all the intellectual and social consequences of the elevation of the Bible into an absolute authority in religion and morality, one can extenuate, even if one can not defend, the claim of some ecclesiastics that the Bible ought not to be put into the hands of the common people. The history of bibliolatry demonstrates quite conclusively that he who seriously and devoutly reads the Holy Scriptures is not invariably led by the Spirit to an understanding of religious truth.

A third means which Protestants have utilized to give content to their freedom is to accept the teachings and character of Jesus as an ultimate norm. Unable to believe the supposition that the Bible is inerrant in all its parts, some Protestants have taken the Bible to be the record of a progressive growth in religious and moral insight, a growth which reaches its culmination in the person of Jesus. This position has the character of combining an entire readiness to accept the results of Biblical scholarship with a reverent piety for the figure which has always been central in Christian thought. It was popular with so-called liberals during the late nineteenth century and part of the present century. Its advocates talked much of "the manhood of the Master," rejecting or at least neglecting speculation concerning Christological problems, plaintively hoping that tender sentiments for a great religious leader would suffice for practical religious purposes and that no one would press questions concerning the cosmic status of this leader. Indeed, they dodged cosmic questions of all sorts, partly perhaps because they were fundamentally skeptics at heart, partly because they dispraised the intellectual life and supposed that therefore the practice of religion was possible without much of any theory to support, interpret, and justify this practice.

This kind of Protestantism is a quite attenuated form of Christianity. Its defenders have been prone to assert that they preferred the religion of Jesus to the religion about Jesus. But historically Christianity has always been a religion about Jesus. The religion of Jesus was Judaism, not Christianity. Jesus, treated as the high point of human development, would yet be a human figure, not the preëxistent Son of God who "was in the beginning with God" and the risen Christ who will come again "to judge the quick and the dead." And if a human figure, he must be studied as any and all human persons ought to be studied, and must be subjected to all the criticisms to which any and all other human persons ought to be subjected. Sentiments of loyalty to him are doubtless suitable as personal preferences by this man or that. But no loyalties to one man, whoever he may be, are capable of being generalized into requirements obligatory on everyone. The Virginian with his loyalty to Robert E. Lee, the American with his loyalty to Abraham Lincoln, the Hindu with his loyalty to Gandhi — these and others with similar admirable personal attachments would never suppose that they had discovered norms of universal import for all races and areas and eras. Why should

Jesus, if he be man, be supposed to be an exception to this quite proper limitation of personal attachments? The devotion proper to Jesus when he is interpreted as the incarnate Son of God is pathetically misplaced when he is viewed as the culmination of religious development among even the most interesting of the ancient races of mankind. It is a vain and perverse liberalism which would reject the Christologies of the historic Christian churches and would yet retain a sentiment toward Jesus which only an orthodox Christology could at all justify. Such a spurious liberalism would turn this sentiment into sheer and inexcusable sentimentality.

Furthermore, the figure of Jesus the Master is by no means clearly and surely known. Those who appeal to him as an authority in religion and morality evidently presume that they can get back of the none too consistent narratives of him in the New Testament to the genuinely historical personage that he actually was. It is questionable how far this presumption can be made good. To orthodox Christianity, Catholic or Protestant, the problem is easily solved; for to the Catholic the interpretation which the Church gives of Jesus, and to the orthodox Protestant the interpretation which the Gospels give of Jesus, is necessarily true. But neither device will serve the needs of the so-called liberal. He must turn historian, weigh evidence, and get at the truth without benefit of revelation either through Church or through text of the New Testament. The earliest of the Gospels in the form in which we have them in the New Testament comes from about A.D. 70. The Gospel according to St. Mark is itself an interpretation of the significance of Jesus rather than a historically minded account of his life. It records the way in which some Christians of about the year 70 regarded Jesus; but it was not written by eyewitnesses nor by disinterested historians. Opinions differ radically today, even among competent scholars, upon the reliability of the Gospel narratives. Those opinions need not be stated and argued here. We need here merely to insist that the so-called liberal, in dodging Christological problems, has become enmeshed in a historical problem which is at least as difficult as the problems he dodged. Lives of Jesus present Jesus in many and incompatible fashions. How can the so-called liberal know which depiction is just? Who indeed is this alleged Master? Are we to take the extremely otherworldly elements in the sayings recorded of Jesus in the Gospels as giving us Jesus' teachings? Or are we to ignore these otherworldly elements and to view Jesus as summoning us to social and economic reforms of our human institutions? Or are we merely to glorify the Master without making clear just what it is of which he is Master? Those who appeal to Jesus as a norm have cultivated a kind of sophisticated inattention to whatever in the written Gospels they do not particularly like. Thus they have done little more than make Jesus in their own image.

The adventure of taking the teachings and character of Jesus as a norm has not been a particularly rewarding form of Protestantism. The seriousness inculcated in men by two cataclysmic world wars has awakened Protestants from the sentimentalism into which some of them were drifting. Men need a religion which grapples more directly and more profoundly with metaphysical and theological questions. But the episode of glorification of Jesus as Master is instructive: it shows the kind of thing which the adventure of Protestantism can become.

A fourth means which Protestants have taken to give content to their freedom may be called, in contrast with the attenuated type just criticized, an amplified Protestantism. It is an effort to take the entire legacy of western culture, even of world culture, and to seek to broaden the base of historic Christianity by using all the instruction which comes from these richer materials. In contrast with the three other means already reviewed, this means does not focus attention upon some one theme which has historically been present in the complex pattern of Catholicism; for the inspiration of the Spirit, the authority of Scripture, and the figure of Jesus are all of them contained, along with much else, in the synthesis of the great Catholic tradition. It is rather the adventure of trying to liberalize the articles of Christian faith by absorbing into them even more extensive materials than historically have ever been included before. In a way, this type of Protestantism has a kind of Catholic intent: it wishes to formulate a great and inclusive norm of faith and sentiment and morals. It is yet genuinely Protestant; for it is not an organized movement but a tendency exhibited by individuals here and there, now and then, without institutional connection and even, normally, without coöperation. Matthew Arnold in England, Emerson in Massachusetts, the Broad Churchmen in the Church of England and the Episcopal Church in the United States, certain of the more literary and scholarly pastors of other denominations — these men have worked for a Protestantism based on a broad human culture. But each has worked alone; and none has received correction or instruction from a consensus among his fellows.

This type of Protestantism, of course, involves more of a break with historic Christianity than does any other type. It has usually appeared in men who, like Matthew Arnold, have realized the spiritual power in what most Christians have scorned as pagan civilization, or, like Emerson, have felt the lure of the culture of the Far East. It has also been frankly experimental or tentative in its forward reachings toward new doctrines, aware that wider understanding of the world and of human cultures will surely require revision of the articles formulated in the past or in the present. It is not nearly so precise in its commitments as other forms of Protestantism; it is still feeling its way, tentatively exploring possibilities, searching for ways to a distant goal.

Protestantism is much more inchoate than Judaism or Catholicism. Judaism is the vehicle for the transmission of a heritage which, since the days of the Diaspora, has been cherished in its integrity rather than developed by further prophetic insights. Catholicism, so far as its essence is concerned, ought never to be fixed and settled; but, in its union with the Romanism of the Roman Catholic Church, it has turned its tradition into dogmas of final authority and has not shown any readiness to expand or revise its fund of teachings. Protestantism alone of the three religious movements has exhibited a supple spirit, a willingness to adapt itself to new knowledge, a friendliness to fresh inquiry and search. If this open-mindedness of Protestantism has led to strange idiosyncrasies, it also gives promise of an ability to lead on to advances in wisdom. It is a valuable element in a world of change, and is the religious correlate of the scientific spirit of experimental investigation. Its errors have been abundant, its weakness is evident, its failures are tragic. But also its opportunity is vast for a future that is quite indeterminate and precarious.

Protestantism in the light of its history can not be regarded as a solution of the nature of Christianity or of religion. It is the posing of a problem rather than a solution. It is the posing of the problem of how freedom, once it is won, may be best used. That is why it may be called an adventure. Its past can not be taken as an indication of what it will come to mean. Circumstances of its history have led it to be too much preoccupied with protesting against external controls and oppressive authorities. Thus hampered, it fell too quickly into premature and immature commitments in its more positive alignments. But if, to the high courage with which Protestants have over and over again dared to assert their freedom, were added more wisdom in using that freedom, the future course of Protestantism might lead into creative adventures of great import for mankind.

V

CONCLUSION

Strange, even ironic, is the history of our religious traditions. Catholic and Protestant have persecuted each other, using torture, the stake, the inquisition. Both have ostracized and abused the Jew; and the Jew, with clannish exclusiveness, has held himself apart from them. Religion, if it has welded groups together in effective unity of purpose, has also cut deep cleavages into the societies of western culture.

Intrinsically, the three central ideas which respectively lie back of the three great religious movements are far from being antagonistic: they are complementary. The hostility of the movements has ensued from factors other than the logic of the ideas. The contrast between the compatibility of the three ideas and the oppositions among the three movements is a reflection upon the seemingly inherent tragedy of human existence. This contrast is enough to justify the plaintive note in the myths which Plato used to describe the world. Ideas, as he was wont to say, become inevitably sullied when they enter into the texture of events, are embodied in matter, and become entangled in the chaotic confusions of space and time. But in themselves and apart from the compromising consequences of their existential careers, ideas are pure, friendly, and coöperative.

When men institutionalize an idea, they make it for the first time an effective and sustained power in the course of events. But they also inevitably involve it in a complex of contending and probably disturbing forces that often pull in directions inconsistent with the idea's genuine intent. The heritage of

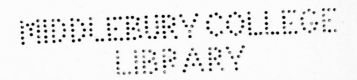

Judaism, when it gained its full development in the noble principle of the Suffering Servant, was the idea of a community of mankind within the moral structure of a sheltering and sustaining covenant. Leadership was not for the aggrandizement of the leaders but for the instruction and elevation of all. Historic Judaism, however, has only partially fulfilled the responsibility of being the channel by which this heritage has been passed along through the centuries. It has, to be sure, been a basic element in the formation of both branches of the Christian faith; and it has operated within the stream of western culture like a leaven, quietly, subtly, sweetly, persuasively, fostering a sense of the integral interdependence of all men, helping so to transform social relationships as to give them heightened dignity and moral enrichment. It has none the less been limited in the execution of its due rôle, not merely by the prejudices and blindness of gentiles to whom it might minister, but also by the biases and narrowness of its own representatives. Orthodox Judaism has been willing to admit only those to a share in its heritage who first accepted such extraneous factors as the rite of circumcision, the celebration of ancient tribal festivals, and conformity to curious dietary regulations. Reform Judaism, in seeking to become thoroughly contemporary and up-to-date, has not been keenly enough aware of its high prerogatives and specific mission. There has not been a large number of Jews who have sympathetically sought to reorient Judaism toward its best latent possibilities.

The same sort of criticism may, indeed must, be brought against the two Christian movements. The vision of Catholicism has been the organization of a body of traditions, moral and cultural, which would maintain, through the vicissitudes of time and change, a steady reliance on a wisdom gleaned from wide and tested human experience. This vision has been the salvation of countless thousands of men who would otherwise have been bewildered by the clash of empires and classes

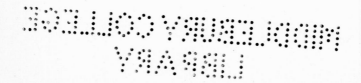

and private desires: it has functioned and still functions with measured success. But hardly had the Church become Catholic than it became also Roman. And in that particular form, it compromised its Catholicity with irrelevant ambitions, such as the quest for temporal power, the supposition that moral authority was the same thing as institutional inerrancy, the conceit that a lesson well learned by men was the very revelation of God and hence above criticism and beyond need of revision. It has confused the laying of a sound foundation on which men might then further build with the preparation of a mold into which human nature was to be poured over and over again as the years pass. Its genuinely Catholic character has been associated with, one can almost say that it has at times been superseded by, a pomp and panoply of gorgeous ceremonies, a display of hierarchical prerogatives, and an ambition to dominate (instead of a hope to improve) the lives of men. If Judaism has moderated too much the purport of its heritage by making it primarily the possession of a chosen few, the Roman Catholic Church has asserted too much the alleged finality of its vision as the sole means of grace for all men.

And the adventure of Protestantism has been the enjoyment of a freedom for personal commitment. This adventure has been the indispensable occasion, not only of escape from many a historic evil, but also, in some cases, of the discovery, or the recovery, of some positive gospel of hope. It has given fresh inspiration to many who were wearied by the reiterated counsels of socially entrenched forces. But its message has frequently been ejaculatory, unbalanced, too insistent upon some partial truth. It has tended to ride some hobby, oblivious of the larger contexts which more organic if less enthusiastic considerations would make clear. It has been adolescent in its intense devotion to some preliminary understanding and in its neglect of the wider ranges of a more comprehensive culture. It has been, to employ a rather harsh epithet from Santayana, a kind of barbarian Christianity. For it has been lacking in sensitiveness to the values of the intellectual and moral legacy which has come down to us from the ancient and medieval worlds. It has gloried too exultantly in a freedom which it has seldom had the experience to utilize with measured wisdom. It has normally detached itself from the achievements of the past, confident that it had, in some one or some few of its favored tenets, sufficient knowledge to enable men to proceed without further support. The cure for its biases may not be, as neo-Thomists and medievalists sometimes assert, a reëstablishment of the world views and cultural controls of the thirteenth century. But some appreciation of traditional values and past human achievements is requisite, if Protestantism's love of adventure is to be more profitably directed; some discipline from our great social heritage is indispensable, if its individualistic assertions are to prove supplementary to the evolving fund of human knowledge and moral principles.

It is theoretically easy to maintain that what we need is an amalgamation of the heritage of Judaism, the genius of Catholicism, and the adventure of Protestantism. The ideas inherent in the three great religious traditions are quite compatible and morally supplementary. Only when a man is nurtured in a wise tradition is he prepared adequately to embark upon fresh adventures; only when a tradition is preserved among people bound together in covenant relation is it truly liberating. Adventure without tradition means chaos; tradition without covenant relation means tyranny. But adventure that occurred on the breeding ground of a great tradition would transform sheer eccentricity into responsible effort for progress; and tradition in the hands of persons who stand in covenant relation would transform pressure for conformity into gracious recognition of a common heritage of culture. The idea of covenant relationship, too, would be enlarged through association with the other two ideas: it would cease to be a tie among persons associated by such accidental factors as race and would become a bond among persons with kindred interests and problems and ideals.

It is also theoretically easy to maintain that, in the United States more than elsewhere, the chances of an association of the three ideas is possible. For America is far from the geographical milieu where strife among the religious organizations was once so bitter and so sustained. Ancient organizations could assume new forms: the essential idea behind the organizations could be preserved while the historical accretions could be eliminated. A new start could be made in the age-old task of freeing the basic principles of human aspiration from the accidents which had arisen around them in the Old World and its partisan quarrels.

What is theoretically easy, however, is often practically quite difficult. Human customs and human passions interfere with logic and reason. And such has been the case with the religious conflicts which were transported from their European home and contentiously continued in the American scene. Antagonisms are thus fostered where coöperative effort is needed. Judaism, Catholicism, and Protestantism remain opposed forces struggling for advantages against one another. The three great religious traditions are still separate possibilities among which men make their choice: they have never been brought together into a moral synthesis. Coöperation among Jews, Catholics, and Protestants has occurred at times, but only on issues that do not affect the separateness of their ancient traditions. Men are seemingly far from understanding how the ideas behind their religious faiths could be so associated that from the distinct contributions of Judaism, Catholicism, and Protestantism could come a unified body of aspiration for the future guidance of mankind.

The causes of separation and strife among the religious traditions are to a great extent matters of administration of the rival institutional interests. And these can be removed, not by discussion, but by the emergence of leaders capable of a higher loyalty than is ever found in devotion to any one of the separate historic faiths. One cause of strife, however, is philosophical rather than administrative. Hence an understanding of this issue might prepare the way for effective union of the three ideas. This philosophical principle is worthy of thorough consideration. It is not a new principle. It has come down to us, like many of the most important philosophical principles of western culture, from the Greeks. It may be called the insight of Hellenism. It is older than either branch of Christianity and is contemporary with some of the finest developments within Judaism. Yet its full import for religion has seldom been realized.

Common to the three religious traditions is the supposition that they rest on revelation from God. To the Jew, the covenant was between Israel and God and was defined by God. To the Catholic, the Church was founded by God and rests upon divine authority. To the Protestant, the means of giving content to his freedom is the voice of God within him or the word of God in the Scriptures or the progressive disclosure of the will of God in history. Division of Jew from Christian and of Catholic from Protestant has made the protagonist of each faith rely with ardent enthusiasm upon his particular way of revelation. And where God speaks or acts, how can man hesitate to put forth his faith with the claim "Thus spake the Lord"? A man who accepts a revelation introduces into the course of events a factor that permits no iota of adjustment to social needs. He may seem, in the psychology of his own conscious processes, to be humbly submitting his private judgment to a higher and infallible power. But he acts, in the social milieu where his faith finds expression, with unyielding assurance and absolutistic finality.

The insight of Hellenism challenges the validity of any and every appeal to revelation. It presents an alternative to the theoretical foundation upon which the three great religious traditions of western culture have commonly sought to build. It therefore involves a radical departure from accepted devices for seeking assurance. It was, however, in its original intent, and it is at all times in its logical bearing upon religious issues, a conservative force in religious affairs. It furnishes a ground for preserving the basic ideas of religious faith from the historic confusions in which they have been entangled.

What, then, is Hellenism, and what is its insight?

Hellenism is a term for that fine flowering of civilization which blossomed among the Greeks in the centuries between Homer and Aristotle. It has in many respects been a rich cultural legacy transmitted from the Greeks to the entire course of western culture. It has been perennially influential. In art and literature, it reached levels of excellence which have enabled men to define standards of merit in these cultural pursuits. In science it made contributions of considerable import: the geometry of Euclid and the speculative presuppositions of the atomism of Democritus are of significance for the more progressive mathematics and physics of recent decades. In religion, too, it has been surprisingly potent, though here its effects are more subtle and difficult to appraise. For, unlike Judaism, Catholicism, and Protestantism, it has had no institution explicitly concerned with its preservation and propagation. It has been sponsored by no priests or clergy who speak expressly for it. It is set forth in no sacred literature, in no creeds, in no set of official doctrines. It has none the less penetrated, sometimes haltingly, sometimes dominantly, into the religious life of Europe and America. It has echoed through Christian literature from St. Augustine and Dante to Emerson and Matthew Arnold. Though it chanced to receive notable, perhaps classic, statement in certain Greek writings, particularly in the Dialogues of Plato, it is not limited in its import to any single culture or to any one tradition. It is, in its bearing upon religion, a technique whereby all religious groups might escape provincialism and become of universal significance.

The religious purport of Hellenism can not be found in an examination of the beliefs and practices of the ancient Greek city-states. Even these beliefs and practices are of more than antiquarian interest. The Eleusinian mysteries have been regarded as furnishing suggestions for the later development of sacramental rites and doctrines in Christendom. The Zeus of Aeschylus offers a parallel to the God of Job. But generally, Greek religious cults had slight bearing on the history of western culture. The goddess Athena, however fair a figure on the Acropolis at Athens, has no meaning for modern Paris or London or Chicago; Poseidon and Ares and Pluto are merely curious to the modern mind.

But Hellenism, it is historically fair to maintain, is not to be identified, even in its religious phases, with the cults of the Olympian deities or with the mysteries. These religious forms survived into the Hellenic period but were not properly its product. They really came from, and derive much of their character from, the wild and barbaric prehistory of the Greeks. In surviving into the Hellenic age they received many cultural transformations and became more civilized in quality, as the Zeus of Aeschylus, just mentioned, instances. Had the Hellenic age not disintegrated in the political subjection and economic catastrophes which ensued upon the death of Alexander, they might even have been fashioned into religious forces of more value for later periods of European history. But at least they are not genuinely Hellenic. What is genuinely Hellenic is the critical spirit which, taking whatever religious beliefs and practices lay about it, sought their ethical purification, their intellectual clarification, their ennoblement. Plato, for example, cared hardly at all whether or not a man believed in Zeus or the other gods; but he cared profoundly what kind of Zeus or other gods a believer in them affirmed. The function of Hellenism, in so far as religion is concerned, is to formulate principles of judgment by which the moral worth and human effect of any and every form of religious worship can be measured. Although Hellenism (in this sense of the term) had of course to operate upon such religions as it found at hand, it is not intrinsically tied up with any of them. It is a critical spirit that is pertinent to any and all religious faiths of any and all ages.

The religious insight of Hellenism can be dramatically set forth in a story which Plato used as the setting for his dialogue *Euthyphro*. Socrates, according to Plato's narrative, had been accused of impiety and had been ordered to appear for trial. On his way to the Athenian court of justice, he met an acquaintance named Euthyphro. This Euthyphro, ironically enough, was approaching the same court with the purpose of bringing the same charge of impiety against his own father. The two men engaged in conversation. Socrates professed ignorance of what piety and impiety are, and asked Euthyphro to tell him. This request Euthyphro confidently agreed to grant. After a few glib but dismal attempts which Socrates quickly exposed as inadequate, Euthyphro proposed to define piety as that which accords with the will of the gods. This dutiful definition, appearing on the surface to be itself quite pious, did not satisfy Socrates. To it Socrates made the rejoinder that the definition dodged a fundamental issue. The polytheistic form of the definition was not what Socrates primarily objected to: a revision of the definition making piety what accords with the will of God would be just as faulty. Socrates' rejoinder penetrated to a deeper issue than the difference between polytheism and monotheism. Do the gods will piety, Socrates asked, because it is pious? Or is piety pious because it is willed by the gods?

The Socratic rejoinder is most emphatically not a play on words. If it seem playful or trivial, the reason may be that it is

posed in terms of the particularity of the ancient charge of
impiety against an Athenian citizen. Released from this particularity and generalized to reveal its full meaning, it raises the
basic problem of the relation between power and value. It
inquires concerning the ultimate before which men ought to
stand in reverence. Is that ultimate a power which, by the very
compulsion of its fiats, creates the distinction between good
and evil? Or is the ultimate rather a value by which all the
powers that there may be, small and great, finite and even in-
finite, may, indeed must, be judged, and to which those powers,
whether they conform or fail to conform to its moral demands,
are alike subject in principle? If it be the former, men and their
consciences are inevitably in bondage to a power against which
protest is not simply useless (because the power may be far
greater than theirs) but even ridiculous (because grounds for
protest are logically void). If it be the latter, men and their
consciences are emancipated from subservience to any and
every existent power, and, at the same time and by that very
fact, are enabled to discriminate among those powers and
thereby to adjust their own loyalties according to these powers' intrinsic worth.

The former alternative has seldom been embraced in its bald
literalness. Calvin is almost the only original and sophisticated
theologian to proclaim it explicitly. Even his most ardent followers generally hedged a bit on the point. But other religious
persons, less aware of the implications of their enthusiasms,
have yet come dangerously near to affirming this alternative
implicitly. Power, when it is vast, fascinates men: it too often
molds their consciences and enslaves their emotions. The very
intensity of religious devotion sometimes robs them of capacity
for just evaluation of the object of their worship, either making them insensitive to the possibility that this object may be
unworthy of worship, or depriving them of the satisfaction of
discerning how and why it may be worthy. Religion is nor-

mally deemed the buttress of morality (and actually has often been such). But when worship has been unhesitatingly lavish, religion has proved to be a force that undermines sound moral judgment.

Examples are not rare of the subversion of morality by religion. Some can be found in the Old Testament. Did not the God of Abraham command him to show a willingness to offer Isaac as a burnt sacrifice? God is portrayed (probably in an editorial revision of the original narrative) as staying the hand of Abraham at the last minute and permitting the substitution of a ram for the son. But the idea is none the less insistently maintained that Abraham was religiously bound to obey God, no matter what God commanded. Similarly, did not the God of David angrily smite Uzzah to death in retaliation for Uzzah's effort to steady the Ark and so to preserve it from falling to the ground? David is reported to have been "displeased" at this exhibition of God's power. But his displeasure, so far as indications in the ancient narrative disclose, was not at the capricious petulance of God. It was rather at the delay which was imposed upon his bringing the Ark successfully to his own house and securing the protection of so powerful a God. These stories are not typical of Old Testament teaching nor of historic Judaism and its lofty ethical development. But they do occur in the text as it has come down to us. They present a view of the relation of God and man which is morally perilous. They contain the idea that God, arbitrary in the exercise of his power, constrains the consciences of men to yield before the terror of his might. They imply the noxious notion that human obligation arises from the fact and the extent of God's power.

This kind of confusion between dominating force and ethical principle is not confined to early and outgrown stages of religion. It reappears unfortunately over and over again in the history of western culture. It occurs in certain forms of recent

Christianity. It is implicit in the attitude of those who thumb the pages of the Bible for texts which will give them ready-made solutions to their moral problems, and also of those who think they are not truly Christians unless they accept every saying of Jesus as binding upon their conduct. The Bible and Jesus are not accepted because their teachings have been critically appraised and found ethically sound; rather, the teachings have been accepted because they are believed to have behind them the power of God. Power is here appealed to as if it were the source of value.

To this alternative and all its insidious variations, Hellenism is firmly opposed. Hellenism accepts joyfully the other alternative, namely, that certain values are in principle supreme, whether or not these values are espoused by powers that sponsor and secure them. If the great values which men may seek are upheld and favored by powers sufficient to make them prevail, then so much the better. For in that case the cosmos is in final analysis friendly to the good, and men are to that extent sustained in their endeavors by a power that makes for righteousness. But if these values are not thus sanctioned, they none the less remain guiding principles for all men of good will. Guarantee of cosmic triumph is not requisite to validity of value. God may be in his heaven or may not be at all; but the worth of the values for which men may properly strive remains in either case unimpaired.

Though Hellenism regards the existence or nonexistence of divine beings as of secondary interest, it is not essentially tied up to skepticism. Doubtless it affords a refuge of which skeptics may take advantage; and, historically, it has at times played into skeptics' hands. But affiliation between Hellenism and skepticism is accidental rather than logically necessary. A convinced advocate of the insight of Hellenism may be a faithful Jew, a devout Catholic, a resolute Protestant, a determined atheist, an honest skeptic. Hellenism is not related to any of these positions as each of them is related to the others: it is not a rival to them as they are rivals of one another. A Hellenist, if he grasps fully the purport of his Hellenism, stands to the positive and historic religions as St. Paul stood to certain religious commitments of his time. He was indeed no skeptic when he wrote to the Christians at Corinth:

Unto the Jews I became as a Jew, that I might gain the Jews; to them that are under the law, as under the law, that I might gain them that are under the law; to them that are without law, as without law . . . that I might gain them that are without law. To the weak became I as weak, that I might gain the weak: I am made all things to all men, that I might by all means save some.

St. Paul was no skeptic: he was dodging no issue. He was putting first things first. So the Hellenist, when he waives the question of the existence of God, is putting first things first. He may believe in God, or he may question or even deny such belief. But to believer and nonbeliever alike, he proclaims that another issue ought to be everyone's primary concern. St. Paul claimed that he stood "without the law," but he refused to let that question divide men. The Hellenist seeks to transcend the differences between theist and atheist by bringing into the foreground an issue in the light of which those differences are of secondary concern. He seeks to bring together into moral unity men who are otherwise estranged by their diverse appeals to revelation. He points out to a believer in God that a prior and major loyalty is due to the value by reference to which the character of God is judged excellent; and to a nonbeliever in God, that similar loyalty is due to that same value, even though the value be nowhere embodied in powers existent in the cosmos.

The insight of Hellenism is not hostile to the treasured faiths of Jew or Catholic or Protestant. Its relation to these faiths is akin to the relation between an American's loyalty to the

United States and his pride in being also a Virginian or Vermonter or Californian. The creation of the United States did not mean the denial of the right of a man to a proper devotion to his local ties; and, as the world becomes increasingly one interrelated whole, loyalty to the common good will not end an American's right to proper devotion to his particular national heritage. But the larger loyalty always demands the termination of isolationism. Hellenism means in religion what internationalism means in politics. A Hellenist who is also Jew or Catholic or Protestant is a man whose traditional religious faith is in process of becoming integrated with other values in an embracing insight. In becoming Hellenists, the Jew and the Catholic and the Protestant would indeed have to abandon many historic trappings of their separate faiths. Their losses, however, would be virtual emancipation from the curious accretions which, in the meandering course of historic events, have gathered around and obscured the central ideas of their great religious traditions. "When I became a man," said St. Paul, "I put away childish things." When a man becomes consciously and genuinely Hellenic, he puts aside the accidental entanglements in which his religious tradition has been caught. He gains moral maturity in loyalty to the larger insight to which his particular religious tradition may indeed be able to make a vital contribution.

Many Jews and Catholics and Protestants may well have been also Hellenists. How many, and who in particular, have been such is a matter to be determined by investigation of the past. That matter is not relevant to the present inquiry. Had all been such, the historic religious traditions would not have been the divisive factors they have frequently been in our western culture. The imperative problem before religious men today is to place the three great historic faiths on a more truly Hellenic basis.

A practical suggestion for progress in religious affairs is to

promote an understanding of the nature of what men eulogisti-
cally call the spiritual life. Too often in the past, tragically
often for the welfare of mankind, the supposition has been
entertained that one can live the spiritual life only after accept-
ing belief in a spiritual world. Belief in a spiritual world is
belief that some spirit exists whose will guides or effectively
participates in the course of events. This belief may be true:
the gods or God may exist. But belief in a spiritual world is
not necessarily productive of spiritual living. It may even en-
slave a man in abject materialism. For if belief in a spiritual
world reconciles a man to acceptance of the course of events
as expressive of God's will, it binds that man morally to submit
to the forces that happen to prevail. And those forces may well
be, indeed sometimes are, immense physical powers and economic greed and lust for domination. Not until and unless
belief in a spiritual world is tempered by Hellenism can that
belief be harmonized with sensitive appreciation of the moral
values toward which men may properly direct their desires.

The spiritual life is life guided by unstinting loyalty to ideal
principles. It can be and has been lived by Jews and Catholics
and Protestants and atheists. It is contingent on no theological
or ecclesiastical or metaphysical commitments. It can well be
lived in a world that is supposedly not a spiritual world at all.
If long ago our world was a swirling mass of physical stuff
without any vestige of life in it; if life originated in some lowly
form of protoplasm; if human life appeared late in a long succession of biological species; if human history is conditioned in
part by physical forces that have no prevision of the outcome
of their existence and their interplay; if men are mortal crea-
tures dependent for their temporary existence upon a delicate
balance of physiological organs and energies; if death termi-
nates each man's existence in turn, and if some physical catas-
trophe might terminate all human life forever — if all this be
true, no threat is raised against the possibility that men may,

here and now, aspire for worthy ends and exhibit heroic loyalty to lofty ideals. The naturalistic world view (to use a term that serves to summarize the various hypotheses just listed) may well be found to have bearing upon the moral choices which men may think they can properly pursue. It may make them keenly aware of the urgency of time and circumstance. It may make them resolve to act zealously for ends within their powers, instead of patiently waiting for the intervention of God to end the evils about them. It may lead them to strengthen the covenant in which they implicitly stand to their fellows, to treasure the wise traditions which they have received from the experiences of those who have lived before them, to embark upon new adventures more maturely (because they can not rely on supernatural aid to rescue them from their improvident moves). It may even inspire them to build a harmonious body of integrated ideals which will combine into effective unity the aspirations of the religious groups about them. It will surely not blind them to the importance of coöperating with those who believe in a spiritual world, but will make them hasten to be the first to express a willingness to preserve and develop the great religious ideas in a culture in which Jew and Gentile, Christian and pagan, alike may share.

Judaism, Catholicism, and Protestantism are too deeply engrained in the habits of men to be superseded by some new-fangled religious institution. They are too intrinsic to the finest aspirations of western culture to be safely abandoned. But they can be refined, and they must be refined, if they are to contribute to an embracing moral program. The obvious means of their refinement is to infuse into them the insight of Hellenism. To the Hellenized Jew, the covenant would be more than a relationship between a racial minority and God: it would be a recognition of the mutual involvement of all men in common problems and common interests and common destinies. To the Hellenized Catholic, the formation of a nurturing tradition would not be limited to the achievement of a particular ecclesiastical body or the prerogative of a particular hierarchy: it would be an enterprise partially accomplished but yet demanding extension, extension even beyond Christendom until western culture gave way gracefully to a world culture of universal import. To the Hellenized Protestant, the content of his freedom would not come from some single strand of his cultural heritage (like the Bible) or some present inspiration of his conscience: it would come through a disciplined understanding of the many yearnings of mankind across the ages. It would then be ready for such revision as might be required by the better understanding of those yet unborn.

Men will probably always appear, as long as there are men who stand in an unbroken continuity of historic developments, who will choose to be Jews, Catholics, and Protestants. The function of Hellenism is not to wean them from these great religious traditions, but to make them more keenly aware of the ideas which those traditions have, even if partially and haltingly, successfully expressed. The history of the great religious traditions enables us to grasp their ideas, but it does not give us any measure of the full import and power of those ideas. Living traditions — and Judaism, Catholicism, and Protestantism are all very much alive today — have a future as well as a past. What those traditions will become depends on how they are adopted and refashioned in each succeeding generation. *What is past, is prologue.*

INDEX

INDEX

Abraham, 11, 87
Adoptianists, 43, 44
Aeschylus, 84
Amos, 14–15
Anabaptists, 61, 67
Apostles' Creed, 41, 42
Archives, Hall of, 7
Aristotle, 83
Arius, 43, 44
Arnold, Matthew, 75, 83; his idea of culture, 4–5
Asceticism in early Christianity, 34
Athanasian Creed, 30, 41–42, 44
Atonement, idea of, 18
Augustine, St., 83

Babylonian influence on Judaism, 9
Barclay, Robert, 68
Bible, its rôle in Protestantism, 69–72; translated into German by Luther, 69; made authoritative by Calvin, Knox, and Presbyterians, 69; bibliolatry, 70–71; uncritical use of, 88
Bibliolatry, 70–71
Bishop, appeal to, as authority, 36
Bryce, James, Viscount, 2

Calvin, appeal to Bible as authority, 69; emphasis on divine power, 86
Canon of New Testament, 36
Catholicism, 3, 30–56, 78–79, 81; nature of, 32–33, 37, 45–46, 52–53; its relation to Romanism, 31–32, 53–55, 79; essential distinction from Protestantism, 60–61; mutual inter-relationships with Protestantism, 62–65; indebtedness to Protestantism, 63; its theory of the Church, 47–49, 50–51; its theory of natural corruption of mankind, 54–55; its idea of original sin, 55; its relations with its mystics, 63; its historic rôle, 78–79

Catholicity, marks of, 51–52; not essentially tied up with Christianity, 32; not exclusively found in the Roman Catholic Church, 32, 56; distinguishable in idea from the Roman Catholic Church, 31–32, 53, 79
Christ, varying beliefs about his person, in the early Church, 38–39; in the fourth century, 42–44. See also Jesus
Church, Catholic theory of its nature, 47–49, 50–51; of its intrinsic holiness, 50–51
Clement I, Pope, 38
Commandment, the first, 13–14
Conservative Judaism, 27
Corruption of mankind, idea of, in the Catholic Church, 54–55
Councils, ecumenical, theory of, 36–37
Covenant, origin of Judaism in, 10–11; distinguished from contract, 11; moral import of, 12; early tribal conception of, 13
Creeds, cause of their development in Christianity, 38–44; practical urgency of, 42; signs of triumph of religion over philosophy, 44–45; the Old Roman Symbol, 41; the Apostles', 41; Nicene, 41–43, 44; Athanasian, 41–43, 44; Westminster Confession, 69–70
Culture, the meaning of, 5–7; Arnold's definition of, 4–6
Cyprian, St., 47–49

Dante, 83
David, King, 13, 87
Decius, Emperor, 46
Democritus, 83
Diaspora, 22–23
Diocletian, Emperor, 49
Donatus, 50

Eleusinian mysteries, 84
Emerson, Ralph Waldo, 75, 83
Erskine, John, 7
Essenes, 18–19, 22, 23
Euclid, 83
Euthyphro, 85–86
Exodus, Book of, 9

Fichte, J. G., 7
Fox, George, 67
Francis, St., of Assisi, 63
Freedom, idea of, in Protestantism, 65
Freedom from authority, in early Christianity, 34

Genesis, Book of, 9
Gnosticism, 40
Greek gods, in contrast with others, 10

Hellenism, its meaning, 83; its essential insight, 82–85, 88–93; its religious function, 85–86; its bearing on Judaism, Catholicism, and Protestantism, 88–90, 93; its opposition to idea of revelation, 82–83; its absence of institutional organization, 83; its theory of the relation of power and value, 88; its accidental connection with skepticism, 88; its idea of the spiritual life, 91–92; its relation to naturalism, 91–92
Heretics, as a coercive factor on the formation of the Christian Church, 44–45; Judaizers, 39–40; Marcion, 40–41; Gnostics, 40; Adoptianists, 43; Sabellius, 43; Arius, 43; Novatian, 47–48; Donatus, 50
History, its uses, 1; its distinction from chronicle, 34
Homer, 83

Ignatius, St., of Antioch, 36
Innocent I, Pope, 38
Isaac, 87
Isaiah, Book of, 16–17
Israeli state, 24

Jesus, a Jew and not a Christian, 21, 72; attack on Pharisees, 20–22; leadership of a reform movement within Judaism, 21–22; written records of his words, 35; unreliability of our historical knowledge about him, 73; erected into a norm by certain Protestants, 71–74, 88. *See also* Christ
Job, Book of, 84
Joshua, 15
Judaism, 3, 4, 8–29, 78, 81; its antiquity, 8; origin in idea of covenant, 10–11; Babylonian influence on, 9; development from monolatry to monotheism, 13–15; its constancy of type, 8–9; its lack of missionary zeal, 8, 27; its confusion of the essential and the extraneous, 25–26; factional divisions within, 18–24; Essenes, 18–19, 22, 23; Zealots, 19, 22–23; Sadducees, 19–20, 22, 23; Pharisees, 20–24; its prophet Jesus of Nazareth, 20–22; purport of the Diaspora, 22–23; Zionism, 24; the Israeli state, 24; Conservative Judaism, 27; Reform Judaism, 27–28; the Jewish problem, 25; problem of the survival of its mission, 25–29; its historic rôle, 78
Judaizers in the early Christian Church, 39–40
Justification by faith in Luther and Protestantism, 66

Kadesh, 9–10, 12

Lapsed, problem of the, 47, 49–50
Luther, Martin, 57, 62, 67; his *Liberty of a Christian Man*, 61–62; his worldly compromises, 61–62; his translation of the Bible into German, 69

Macaulay, Thomas B., 53
Maccabees, 19
Marcion, 40–41
Mark, Gospel according to St., 73
Matthew, Gospel according to St., 21

Monolatry, 13–14
Monotheism, growth of, among the Jews, 13–15, 17
Moses, 9–10, 12

Newman, John Henry, 3
Nicene Creed, 41–42, 44
Novatian, 47–48

Old Roman Symbol, 41
Original sin, idea of, 55

Paul, St., 34, 35, 89, 90
Persecutions, Roman, of Christianity, 46–51
Pharisees, their religious position, 20; picture of them in the New Testament, 20–21, 23; relation to Jesus, 20–22; historic channel of transmission of Judaism, 22–24; triumph over other Jewish sects, 23–24
Plato, 2, 77, 83, 85
Progress, conditions for religious, 90–91
Prophets, of Israel, 12
Protestantism, 3, 4, 57–76, 79–80, 81; its essential character, 65–66; two meanings of the verb to protest, 59–60; its spread, 57–58; its affiliations with the modern temper, 58; its lack of unity, 58–59; its individualism, 60–61; not essentially tied up with Christianity, 62; distinguished in character from Catholicism, 60–61; mutual interrelationships with Catholicism, 62–65; indebtedness to Catholicism, 64–65; its problem of freedom, 65–66; its appeal to the Spirit, 66–67; its appeal to the Bible, 69–70; its appeal to the historic Jesus, 71–74; superficiality of liberal Protestantism, 72–74; the chaotic nature of, 75–76; its problem and its promise, 76; its historic rôle, 79–80

Quakers, 67–69

Reform Judaism, 27–28
Reinvestiture of the clergy, 49–50
Revelation, historic influence of the claim to, 82; and Hellenism, 82–83
Roman Catholic Church, a union of Catholicity and Romanism, 30–32, 53
Romanism, its relation to Catholicism, 31–32, 53–55, 79; its origin and growth, 37; superimposed upon the Catholic Church, 33, 53; its growing rigidity, 63–64

Sabellius, 43–44
Sacraments, problem of the validity of, 50–51
Sadducees, 19–20, 22, 23
Santayana, George, 79
Shakespeare, William, 60
Socrates, 85
Spinoza, Baruch, 18
Spirit, the appeal to, in St. Paul and the early Christians, 34; by Luther and Protestantism, 66–67; by Anabaptists, 67; by Quakers, 68
Standards, quest for, in the early Christian Church, 35–37
Suffering Servant, idea of, 16, 78

Theresa, St., 63
Tradition, its meaning and rôle, 6–7; its value, 80
Trent, Council of, 42

Underhill, John, 68
Uzzah, 87

Westminster Confession, 69–70

Yahweh, 9–17

Zealots, 19, 22, 23
Zionist movement, 24